Parting Words/ Parting Ways

Saying Good-Bye to Your Pet

Laura Ritter Carlson

LOST
COAST
PRESS

Thank you for caring about our animal angels —

Laura R Carlson

Parting Words / Parting Ways:
Saying Goodbye to Your Pet
Copyright © 2002 by Laura Ritter Carlson

Lost Coast Press
155 Cypress Street
Fort Bragg, California 95437
(707) 964-9520
Fax: 707-964-7531
http:\\www.cypresshouse.com

Cover Design: Gopa Illustration and Design
Cover Art: Paula Teplitz
Author Photo with "Baci" by Mark Carlson

Library of Congress Cataloging-in Publication Data
Carlson, Laura Ritter, 1959 -
  Parting words / parting ways : saying good-bye to your pet / Laura Ritter Carlson. – 1st ed.
    p. cm.
  ISBN 1-882897-62-5 (pbk)
  1. Pet owners -- Psychology. 2. Pets–Death–Psychological aspects.
3. Bereavement -- Psychological aspects. 4. Pet owners--Correspondence.
I. Title.
  SF411.47 .C37 2002
  155.9'37–dc21   2001029291

Book production by Lost Coast Press
Proceeds from the sale of this book will be donated to Animal Welfare.

2   4   6   8   9   7   5   3

Printed in Canada

Permissions

Acknowledgments

My thanks to:

Mark, for his unwavering confidence in me, but especially for a comment I overheard him make to our large animal vet: that he never knew he was a "cat person" until he met me. (My purpose has been recognized.)

Lola and Ken Ritter, for allowing Sandra, Lynne, Cheryl, Ken and me to keep Samantha, adopt Cher and to grow up instilled with their own love and respect for animals. For patiently (and repeatedly) listening to Maggie bark "cookie" into the phone and acting suitably impressed. To Dad for instilling in me motivation and belief in myself, and to Mom for showing up to surprise me and her grandkittens, Thomas and Trinket, on their adoption day at the shelter.

Susan Carlson, for reminding me of the selflessness of animals and that one leaves us so that another may know the joy and love we have to share.

Frank Spear, for sharing his photographs, which mirror his respect, appreciation and love for all animals.

Doris and Mel Carlson, who, when they call on the phone, never fail to ask who's new in the household.

John P. Griffin, DVM and Carla Rasmussen, DVM and the caring staff of Evergreen Animal Hospital for their expertise, knowledge and deep respect for the human/companion animal bond. And to E.B. Okrasinski, DVM, the orthopedic surgeon they called upon, for his honesty regarding surgical options and for replying to my comment that I couldn't just watch Chance's health fail and do nothing, by telling me that I would be doing a lot by keeping him as comfortable as possible for as long as possible. Thank you for that empowerment in a situation in which I felt helpless.

Jonathan Wright, DVM for his willingness to help Chance with homeopathic medicine. You gave us some additional time together, which I believe helped me come to terms with the inevitable.

Laurel Wright, DVM, for her time and patience when I went to her with Chance's MRI in my attempts to "save" him. Thank you for what I realize now as grief counseling. I wouldn't have been able to acknowledge it as such at the time.

Jaida, Chance, Annie, and Mouse for preparing me for all the four-legged family members I have yet to meet by teaching me that I can love them and still say goodbye.

Sprite, who graciously allowed me space in "her" home office at all hours of the day and night.

Smidge, for showing me how wonderful adopting an adult pet can be.

Maggie, for her company as she stretched out under the computer desk, also known as her indoor doghouse.

Sheba, our rescued donkey, for proving me right when I repeatedly told her that I had more patience than she had distrust.

Hannah, our cat who thinks she's a dog, for allowing others to share her castle and graciously greeting all who enter therein.

Holly, for being the best gift Annie could ever have given us.

Thomas and Trinket, who took turns playing "catch the cursor," sleeping in my lap and using the keyboard in attempt to add their opinions to the book.

And Baci, who came to us toward the completion of this book. You are a shining example of what tremendous strength and spirit can be housed in such a fragile body. You are my survivor.

Mostly, my sincere and heartfelt thank you to everyone who submitted a letter to their pet, making this world-wide support system possible. With words this touching, I have to believe that they were heard beyond this realm.

Foreword

Written by Jack Davies, one of the original founders of the Humane Society of America, and its first Director of Public Relations, and his wife Mary Ann, who together own and operate Dog Haven, a no-kill shelter for homeless, ill and injured dogs of Puerto Rico (Dog Haven, Inc., POB 1122, Utuado, PR 00641).

*Y*ears ago I had the honor of participating with Clifton Fadiman in the World Federalist Foundation and in those years also helped found the Humane Society of America. I still feel those two organizations, the World Federalist which sadly did not come to fruition, and the Humane Society which has made many positive contributions to the consideration of and care for animals over the years, to be connected.

We are at the threshold of the new century and the necessities of world peace are ever pressing. The relationship between all forms of life all over our wonderful planet is more a necessity now than it ever has been.

Our little farm, Dog Haven, is a tiny participant in this coexistence. Over the some seventeen years of its existence we have loved and cared for countless numbers of animals, mainly canines, but also needy horses and very special cats, as well as three goats, two geese and a number of other fowl.

We feel we have made, and are continuing to make, a positive contribution to our community and in a certain way to the world.

This book is a tribute to the special bond that forms between animals and their people. It is a book that will do immeasurable good for those who read it and has done so already for those who have shared their experiences here. It is heartening to know how deeply the animals presented in these pages were loved and that they live on in the minds and hearts of their families. It is a testament to the positive experiences that occur in our world. We're glad to be a small part of the experience.

Introduction

*H*ave you lost a much-loved pet? Whether suddenly, due to an accident or an acute illness or gradually, due to old age, it is never easy to say good-bye to a loved one. Euthanasia and the disappearance of a pet can be particularly heartbreaking issues. While the reason for your loss may vary, the sorrow is still as real and can be just as painful.

This collection of letters is designed to help people, readers as well as writers, not only deal with the loss of their pets, but honor them at the same time. These letters are personal and lasting tributes to our special friends and in sharing them we hope that we, along with our pets, can help others heal.

Having written a letter to my dog, Chance, the day before I had to help him leave this life and his pain behind, I realized how cathartic it had been at the time and how healing it had become in the months and years to follow. It helped to have a remembrance of my feelings at that point in our lives and the jumble of emotions I'd faced. Writing the letter, I never imagined I would ever share it with anyone but Chance. It is tied with a ribbon and buried with him, next to his heart. It took almost three years of unending, almost obsessive research on pet loss and grieving, investigating theories regarding life after death, pet/human heaven and pet loss counseling training for me to realize that by sharing Chance's letter we could help others. Response to the web site invitation for others to write letters and join Chance and me in our efforts was overwhelming and beautiful.

In these pages you'll meet people ages thirteen to eighty-eight and their special animal friends. By reading the letters they've written to them, you'll learn how deeply the loss of a pet can be felt. Whether these people and pets were together for a few weeks or many years, the common thread underlying each relationship is the bond they will always share. By joining together and sharing our letters we hope to let other people know that they are not alone in their grief and mourning.

Initially, I wondered about the ramifications of being involved in such a potentially depressing project, however, the exact opposite has proven to be true. The animals honored in these pages were, and will always be, loved and cherished. They had the chance to enjoy the comforts of a warm home and loving family. They worked their pure, innocent and honest animal-magic to leave lasting impressions upon people's hearts and change their lives forever.

While this collection inevitably brought some tears, during both the writing and the reading, in its final form it has become an uplifting, heartwarming tribute recognizing and honoring the bond we share with our pets.

I hope that in sharing these letters we will help others, as well as ourselves, not only deal with pet loss, but honor our beloved companions in the lasting and open way they deserve to be remembered.

Our pets live on inside of us. No matter how long they are with us, they become a part of who we are; usually the best part. They teach us throughout our time here together, and we develop and change and grow from what we learn. With this collection of letters, our pets will be allowed to live on, teaching, and we hopefully can go on, learning.

Contents

Acknowledgments   v

Foreword   vi

Introduction   vii

Anonymous Poem   x

Five Stages of Grief   1

Poem for the Grieving   3

Five Steps in Healing   4

God's Promise   6

Children and Grief   8

Pets and Grief   9

Prayer   10

Preparing for Loss—Euthanasia   11

Unexpected or Sudden Loss   13

When the Time Comes   14

Burial or Cremation   15

Memorial Services and Funerals   16

Poem   17

Memorializing Your Pet   18

Memories   21

Rainbow Bridge   22

Cats   23

Dogs   77

Other Friends   203

My Forever Friend   230

Dedication

*T*o Chance, my main inspiration for this book. I know you were right beside me with every letter I read and every word I wrote. We've made many friends in these pages, and I feel that I've met some of the people whose animals you are now friends with at Rainbow Bridge.

Our animals shepherd us through certain eras of our lives.
When we are ready to turn the corner
and make it on our own ... they let us go.

— author unknown

Five Stages of Grief

Realizing that the grieving process can generally be divided into stages may ease the confusion of dealing with loss. Not everyone passes through each stage in a set order, nor does everyone experience each stage for an equal time.

For example, one person may spend more time in denial, jump to bargaining, then experience anger for quite a while before entering depression and then finally accepting the loss. Another may start with depression and feelings of helplessness, which may lead to attempts at bargaining and the realization it is not going to work, then progress to anger and acceptance. One stage or some stages may be skipped entirely.

There is a myriad of possibilities and combinations. No one way is right or wrong. Let yourself progress through the grieving process however it comes naturally because you will inherently find your own best path.

1. *Shock and Denial*: The bereaved may feel confused and over-whelmed. The loss or impending loss can feel unreal and thus difficult to accept.
2. *Anger and Guilt*: The bereaved may feel anger toward an "unjust" world, which may include family, friends, other pets, doctors or God. Often guilt is directed at themselves for what they perhaps could have, or should have done.
3. *Bargaining*: Bargaining with God, themselves or making general promises to be a "better person," for example, may govern a person's feelings in this stage.
4. *Depression*: Losing a loved one may create a sense of major change in lifestyle. The daily dog-walks, the cat who slept next to you each night, even a pet's feeding or medication schedule can become routine and anticipated each day. This stage may include feelings of intense sadness, loneliness, emptiness and futility.
5. *Acceptance*: Acceptance can be realized when the changes created by the loss are fit into an adjusted lifestyle. People handle this stage in individual ways. Much depends on the relationship of the pet and person, the circumstances surrounding the loss such as whether it was sudden like an accident or injury, or a long-term disease or illness, whether other pets or people live in the household, and whether the bereaved has an understanding and sympathetic support system. Our pets teach us to be adaptable and flexible, and these are qualities that will help you heal.

It doesn't matter where you happen to begin, or in what order you progress through the grief process, but rather that you acknowledge and validate your feelings through the entire experience. In this way you can find healing.

A Poem for the Grieving

Do not stand at my grave and weep.
I am not there, I do not sleep.
I am a thousand winds that blow,
I am the diamond glints on snow.
I am the sunlight on ripened grain,
I am the gentle autumn's rain.
When you awaken in the morning's hush,
I am the swift uplifting rush
of quiet birds in circled flight.
I am the stars that shine at night.
Do not stand at my grave and cry,
I am not there. I did not die...

—author unknown

Five Steps in Healing

*P*ets are our children, friends, companions, confidants. Perhaps you regard your pet as a substitute parent because you feel accountable to the animal and strive to meet whatever expectations you believe him to have of you. Much depends on your own upbringing and socialization in defining your relationship with your pet. Regardless of this, however, we view them as someone who offers unconditional love and nonjudgmental loyalty. They give us a reason to get up in the morning and come home at night. Because they create a purpose in our lives, we incorporate our pets into our daily schedules. They give us deep appreciation for filling basic needs similar to ours, such as clean water, food and warmth, both physical and emotional.

To lose such a relationship can be like losing a parent, child, sibling and best friend all at once. It is no wonder that we mourn the loss of a pet so deeply and can have a difficult time coming to terms with it.

1. Give yourself permission to mourn your loss. You loved your pet and shared a special relationship. You have the right to grieve. Only you know how long you should mourn and how you should go about it.

2. Be extra special to yourself by following your daily schedule as closely as possible. Stay well-hydrated, well-rested, exercise moderately and eat well.

3. Find a support system, whether with family, friends, group meetings or individual counseling. Talk with people who understand and empathize with you. This is no time to feel you have to justify your grieving to anyone.

4. Memorialize your pet. Acknowledge and honor what he or she

meant, and still means, to you. Express yourself through writing, art, meditation, photography, gardening, music, volunteer work or even adoption of another pet.

5. Forgive yourself if you slip backwards occasionally. Grief can be triggered by a song, a holiday, family vacation time, passing the pet food aisle at the store or finding pet hairs on the couch or a toy under the cushion. Realize that you'll have "good" days and "not-so-good" days, and allow yourself both.

God's Promise

God promised at the birth of time,
A special friend to give.
His time on Earth is short, He said,
So love him while he lives.
It may be six or seven years
Or twelve or then sixteen.
But will you, till I call him back,
Take care of him for me?
A wagging tail and cold wet nose
And silken velvet ears,
A heart as big as all outdoors,
To love you through the years.
His puppy ways will gladden you
And antics bring a smile,
As guardian or friend he will
Be loyal all the while.
He'll bring his charms to grace your life
And though his stay be brief,
When he's gone the memories
Are solace for your grief.
I cannot promise he will stay
Since all from earth return,
But lessons only a dog can teach
I want you each to learn.

Follow his lead and gain a life
Brim full of simple pleasure.
Whatever love you give to him,
Returns in triple measure.
Enjoy each day as it comes,
Allow your heart to guide,
Be loyal and steadfast in love
As the dog-child at your side.
Now will you give him all your love,
Nor think the labor vain,
Nor hate me when I come to call
To take him back again.
I fancy each of us would say,
Dear Lord, thy will be done,
Before all the joy this dog shall bring,
The risk of grief we'll run.
We'll shelter him with tenderness,
We'll love him while we may,
And for the happiness we've known,
Forever grateful stay.
But shall the angels call for him
Much sooner than we've planned,
We'll brave the bitter grief that comes,
And try to understand.

—author unknown

Children and Grief

Children tend to grieve for a shorter period than adults, reaching the "acceptance" phase sooner. However, their grief may be more intense due to lack of understanding. The death of a pet may be a child's first experience in dealing with loss, so expect questions from simple to complex.

1. Discuss openly the death of the pet in terms that do not sugar-coat the loss. Saying that the animal was "put to sleep" may create a fear of going to bed at night. It's important to be straightforward in your discussions because children tend to take comments very literally. Explain as simply and honestly as possible the concepts of illness and old age.

2. Inform teachers and caregivers of the loss so they won't be surprised by any questions about death or dying. It will also make them aware of the probable reason for any mood changes or behavior differences.

3. Encourage the child to create his or her own memorial for the pet, decorating a frame for a special photograph of them together, drawing a picture of play time together, or recording favorite memories on an audiocassette or compact disc.

4. Because children tend to verbally return to a subject that's weighing on their mind, expect the topic to come up repeatedly for a while and be patient and tolerant.

Pets and Grief

Surviving pets may experience reactions amazingly similar to a person's, such as anxiety, depression and sleep disturbances. Animals can form strong bonds with one another, and even if they appear outwardly not to be the best of friends, they may still grieve. They may search for the missing pet, cry, assume some of the missing pet's mannerisms or quirks, and seek extra attention from you.

1. Keep the animal's daily routine as normal as possible. Don't change food, bedding or schedules.
2. Give them lots of attention and affection, but be careful not to overcompensate, which may result in eventual separation anxiety.
3. You can help surviving pets through this difficult time by being patient, gentle and kind. They are perceptive and impressionable and can sense moods intuitively. Remember, they are dealing with their own sense of loss and change, and how you manage your grief can set the tone for their reactions. Response to loss is likely to vary from pet to pet, just as it does from person to person.
4. Don't adopt a new playmate for the surviving pet unless both of you are ready. Give everyone time to adjust and accept the loss so that resentments aren't formed toward the new pet. It takes energy to grieve and time to heal. Allow everyone in the household these luxuries at their own rate.

Prayer

Bless Thy beasts
And singing birds
And guard with tenderness
Small things that have no words.

Preparing for Loss – Euthanasia

*W*hile you can try to "prepare" as much as possible for the antici-pated loss of an ill or elderly pet, the reality won't sink in until after the animal is gone. The house feels empty and your daily routine is altered. Making certain decisions ahead of time can somewhat ease the burden you feel afterwards and hopefully help you through your grief.

1. Understand the concepts of loss and grief and know which family members and friends you can turn to for unfailing support and understanding. You may even want to speak to a grief counselor while your pet is ill or failing, rather than waiting until after he is gone.

3. Make a written list of factors that would negatively affect your pet's quality of life so you will know if it comes time to opt for euthanasia. Some determining factors may be incontinence, lack of appetite, constant pain, or unresponsiveness to surroundings, attention or affection. Honor your list.

4. Write down your desires ahead of time, regarding burial or crema-tion, funeral or memorial service and how you'd like to memorial-ize your pet. Talk to your veterinarian about euthanasia options such as being present during the procedure or having it done at your home. Some veterinarians will perform the procedure at a client's car in the clinic parking lot in an effort to lessen the pet's stress or if mobility is a problem. Consider what would be least traumatic for your pet, as well as yourself.

5. Trust yourself and your decisions. Your pet does. While your vet-erinarian can assess his physical condition, you are the best judge

of his quality of life. Taking both these factors into consideration, you have the capability of sparing your pet misery, pain and suffering. Euthanasia literally means "good death."

It may initially seem morbid or disloyal to plan ahead like this, but in reality, you will be making the transition much smoother and easier for both you and your pet. You will most likely be dazed and distraught when you actually lose your pet and therefore not in a frame of mind capable to make such decisions. Thinking ahead will inevitably spare you more heartache later.

Unexpected or Sudden Loss

Sometimes we are not permitted time to prepare for, or even anticipate, the loss of a pet. In cases of traumatic loss such as from a motor vehicle injury, animal attack or accident, the sense of loss can be more dramatic because it is so unexpected. This is where your spirituality can play a large role.

Rather than trying to justify the loss, it may be emotionally gentler if you attempt to understand it. The difference between the two is that it can be initially difficult, while still in shock, to try to justify how such a thing could happen. By trying to understand, you are brought little closer to acceptance.

Understanding can mean believing that everything happens for a reason, although the reason may not be apparent at the time. Perhaps the accident spared the animal from a worse, lingering death. Maybe the incident brought certain family members closer or made you reach out to people who needed you as much as you needed them. Perhaps you'll feel led to speak to the public to educate about a particular pet hazard or danger, or it made you more aware of how you can keep your other pets safer.

When the Time Comes

If it should be that I grow frail and weak,
And pain should keep me from my sleep,
Then will you do what must be done,
For this, the last battle, can't be won.
You will be sad I understand,
But don't let grief then stay your hand,
For on this day, more than the rest,
Your love and friendship must stand the test.
We have had so many happy years,
You wouldn't want me to suffer so
When the time comes, please let me go.

Take me to where my needs they'll tend,
Only...stay with me till the end.
And hold me firm and speak to me,
Until my eyes no longer see.
I know in time you will agree,
It is a kindness you do for me.
Although my tail its last has waved,
From pain and suffering I have been saved.
Don't grieve that it must be you,
Who has to decide this thing to do;
We've been so close, we two, these years,
Don't let your heart hold any tears.

—author unknown

Burial or Cremation

Regarding disposal of the body, you have several options. It is helpful to check them out ahead of time so that you can make an informed decision that you feel comfortable with, and have plans in place.

If you have the space and your city allows you to bury your pet's body at home, you may want to create a little garden area for this purpose. However, if your present home is leased or rented, you may not have the legal right to bury your pet there, and you may want to ask permission. You may also want to consider burial in a pet cemetery. This way you can have peace of mind knowing where your pet is, no matter where you live.

Cremation destroys any disease or bacteria in an animal's body and thus will not contaminate an area if you decide to scatter, bury or keep the cremains. One option is a private cremation in which you could have the ashes of your pet. Another option is a mass cremation in which your pet would be cremated along with other animals. Some people make arrangements for their pet's cremains to be buried with them at the time of their own death.

You may ask your veterinarian for assistance in disposing of the body. In some cases, as with many animal shelters, the body is sent to a rendering facility rather than a mass cremation or mass burial.

Memorial Services and Funerals

*I*f your pet's health is failing you may want to have a get-together before the actual passing so that people can honor his life at that time. Some pets, more than others, may enjoy the attention and comfort of familiar friends and family around them. You are the best judge of his preferences and comfort level at this often difficult stage of life.

If you opt to scatter ashes at a favorite place such as the mountains or beach, or if friends and family cannot attend a ceremony, send a note informing of the service and ask that people take a few moments at a specified time to remember your pet.

If gathering at the actual burial, you may want to invite people to bring a note, poem, photograph or other special remembrance of your pet to share and perhaps bury with him. Some people may want to say a few words, a prayer, sing a song or hymn or play some music. Others may need quiet time for thoughts and memories.

Headstones, grave markers and urns may be purchased from companies specializing in such products specifically for pets.

Honoring your pet's life and remembering your time together is the most important element, whether you choose to do so with an elaborate ceremony, a private service or a few quiet moments to yourself. Simply acknowledging the bond you shared and recognizing what this loss means to you is a constructive part of the healing process, and how you decide to do so is a personal preference.

In one of the stars
I shall be living.
In one of them
I shall be laughing.
And so it will be
as if all the stars
were laughing,
when you look at the sky at night…

—The Little Prince

Antoine de Saint-Exupéry

Memorializing Your Pet

*B*ecause a memorial will hopefully help you personally deal with the difficult issue of losing or having already lost your pet, you may honor a pet who is ailing or one who has already passed on. Because "loss" doesn't always mean "death," it may help to honor a pet who perhaps just disappeared one day, or one given up in a family separation.

Memorializing your pet will not only help you deal with your loss, but honor your beloved companions in the lasting and open way they deserve to be remembered.

These are gifts you can give to your pet, as well as yourself.

Adopt

The timing for bringing another animal into your life is a personal decision. Recognize that you have a beautiful gift to be able to love an animal so much that you feel the pain of the loss so deeply. Give that love to another pet. Share your home and heart with another animal to honor the memory of the one you lost. The highest compliment we can offer a pet we've lost is to open our heart to another one so that he, too, can experience what having a safe home and loving family really means. Thinking you can "replace" your pet will inevitably lead to comparisons and disappointments, but the void may be filled by opening up to another animal, who will be loved and appreciated for his own personality.

Art

- Create a stepping stone from kits available in art supply stores. Use as a grave marker.

- Make an imprint of your pet's paw using a kit made for this purpose.

• Use calligraphy to remember a poem that reminds you of your pet, or write your own.

• Draw, paint or make a collage representing what your pet means to you.

• Fill a shadow box frame or glass-topped display table with collar, tags, a favorite toy, a piece of blanket and a photograph.

• Design and print a memorial announcement, perhaps with photo, to mail to friends and family and veterinarians who understand your loss.

Commission a Memorial

Have an artist reproduce your pet's photograph on a ceramic tile, art canvas, laser-cut wooden box or wooden photo album cover. These services are available in many gift catalogs or you may find willing talent at an artists' co-op in your area. You can also have a photo reproduced on a pillow, t-shirt, sweatshirt, mousepad, plate or coffee cup, usually at your neighborhood drugstore or photo developing shop. Here, too, your imagination is your guide.

Donate

Make a donation in your pet's name to an animal shelter or rescue group. Give pet food, towels, blankets, toys, or volunteer your time. Shelters often have volunteers who visit schools to teach students how to avoid dog bites or how to properly care for pets. Detention centers and youth prisons may welcome speakers to share information about the proven link between animal abuse and violent crimes against humans.

Gardening

• Plant an annual.

• Have a garden marker or grave site marker engraved.

• Create a memorial site with flowers, statues, a bench, fountain, whatever brings you peace.

Meditation

Clear your mind, listen to instrumental music or a sounds-of-nature tape, walk, exercise, do yoga. Allow yourself an escape into relaxation.

Music

Make a tape or CD of songs that remind you of your pet. Listen to calm, soothing music, which has been shown to lower blood pressure and ease anxiety, similar to the effects of stroking a animal.

Photography

Compile a photo album, fill frames with favorite photos, or wear a locket or photo-pin to carry your pet's picture or hair with you.

Video

Edit home videos into a collection of memories on tape. The same can be done with still photographs by having them transferred to videotape so you can sit back and watch memories of your pet's life with you.

Writing

A letter, poem, story or collection of favorite memories can help you remember how your pet helped you through a difficult phase of your life or shared the best time of your life...or both, as is often the case. Your letter may be written as a thank you, a remembrance, an apology, a good-bye. How did he or she touch your heart? Change your outlook on something? Teach you one of life's lessons? The key is that your letter is just that...your letter to your special friend.

While it will undoubtedly bring some tears, your memorial will be, in its final form, a compilation of your love and memories acknowledging and honoring the bond you and your pet will always share.

Memories

We little knew that morning,
God was going to call your name.
In life we loved you dearly,
In death we do the same.
It broke our hearts to lose you,
You did not go alone,
For part of us went with you,
The day God called you home.
You left us beautiful memories,
Your love is still our guide,
And though we cannot see you,
You are always by our side.
The family chain is broken,
And nothing seems the same,
But as God calls us one by one,
The chain will link again.

—author unknown

Rainbow Bridge

There is a bridge connecting Heaven and Earth. It is called the Rainbow Bridge because of its many colors. Just this side of the Rainbow Bridge, there is a land of meadows, hills and valleys with lush green grass.

When a beloved pet dies, the pet goes to this place. There is always food and water and warm Spring weather. Those old and frail animals are young again. Those who have been maimed are made whole again. They play all day with each other.

There is only one thing missing. They are not with their special person who loved them on Earth.

So each day they run and play until the day comes when one suddenly stops playing and looks up. The nose twitches! The ears are up! The eyes are staring! And this one suddenly runs from the group.

You have been seen, and when you and your special friend meet, you take him or her in your arms and embrace. Your face is kissed again and again and again, and you look once more into the eyes of your trusting friend. Then you cross the Rainbow Bridge together, never again to be separated.

—author unknown

Cats

To anyone who has ever been owned by a cat,
it will come as no surprise that there are all sorts of things
about your cat you will never, as long as you live, forget.

—Cleveland Amory

ANNIE

DOMESTIC SHORTHAIR CAT, GREY TABBY & WHITE
11-YEAR-OLD FEMALE
JUNE 1987 - AUGUST 8, 1998

Dear Annie,

When I think of you, the sweetest, most gentle friend comes to mind. You are without a doubt such an accepting, easygoing and loving cat. The past two days and nights I've prayed for a miracle, which is now what it would take to make you the happy little kitty you were. But your heart is failing and the problem is irreversible. If there was any chance it could be turned around, I would give it to you.

Annie, I know you are hanging on now…for me. But it's time to let go. I told you when I had to leave you at the emergency hospital that night, that if you had to go, it was okay, but you hung on and when the phone rang in the morning, I knew you'd made it through the night. At your veterinarian's office the next morning, he said you were a tough cat. You really are. And you also have a gentle, loving soul. But it's okay to go now. You deserve to be out of pain and in a better place spiritually. I will help you go because I love you so much.

I'll miss you sleeping on my shoulder, an endearing habit I think you picked up since we moved into this house. I'll miss the warmth of your body on my back and shoulder and the comfort of your purr in my ear. You lulled me to sleep many nights. Sometimes if you fell asleep before I did, I'd gently shrug my shoulder and you'd begin to purr again. You were always my comfort. You brought us a lot of joy, Annie. And your memories will, still.

I'll be with you today, Annie, when you slip away to your own sleep where I promise you, comfort awaits. You'll see Chance and Jaida again. You won't hurt anymore. You'll be safe. You'll be able to do whatever you want, and you'll be content. I already miss you terribly, but we'll be together again one day.

I love you to the sky, my little Annie-Cat.

Laura

AVERY

MAINE COON MIX
5-YEAR-OLD MALE
APRIL 13, 1993 - JULY 7, 1998

Dear Avery,

It is so hard to believe it has been almost a year since that morning when I held you for the last time. There are so many things I would have done or said if I had known I would never take you home again.

I can still hear your Daddy's words while I was putting on my make up. "Honey, something's wrong with Avery." Silly me, I thought you were sick from the pizza you had stolen from the counter the night before. Still, I packed you up and took you to the vet. To the last place on earth you wanted to be. We worked so hard to try to save you, and you worked so hard to get away. Avery, I hope now you know I only wanted to do all I could to keep you here with us, with your family. I know then it seemed like torture and I hope you know the scars on my arms have faded now and Mommy was never angry when you bit me. I know you were just scared.

I like to think of you now doing all the things that were so hard for you here. I hope you are running without the shortness of breath that came with the asthma and heart disease that took you from us. I hope they have a big giant "ratman" toy and you sleep on him every night. Most of all I hope you found a lap to lie on and a soft thigh to knead. I hope your purr, that was so tentative and long coming here is as loud as an engine now. I think of your soft fur and your bright green eyes every day still. You were a stately gentleman for the brief time you were with us.

You did so much for us, Avery. Every night when we went to bed, you got up and stood guard at the windows, paced in front of the doors, and ushered your seven brothers and sisters around in the safety of your shadow. You were a thirteen-pound guard cat of the highest order. You taught your feline siblings what it meant to be a cat. They miss being held down by your giant paws and washed behind the ears. Well, Alexis does not miss it, but you probably know that. There is no one to walk into the litter boxes now and do an inspection and cover up all the mess. I guess I do that for you now. But Avery, they still sit and wait to eat their food until everyone is served. (And you thought they were barbarians!) I think they are still waiting for you.

Taz cried for you every night until we got your ashes back. I guess he did not like the idea that even for four days I had turned you over to strangers. He knew how you would hate that. He often sleeps next to your picture and the little memorial we made for you. But I know, like your father and I, he would rather have you back. I wish you could see all the wonderful things you gave us in those all too brief years. You gave us unconditional love, laughter, memories, safety, and what was hardest for you, you gave us your trust. We are so grateful for that Avery.

I only wanted to tell you to have a good time at Rainbow Bridge, to watch for us and to please be there for your brothers and sisters when their time comes. For your father and I will never worry about them. They will walk in the shadow of our Silver Tabby guard cat. Please do not worry about your father and me. We are a little sadder without you, but we have your lifetime of memories to guard our hearts. We love you "Aveman Caveman." Don't forget to wash behind your ears.

Love,
Kathy

Kathy Nguyen
Professional Pet Sitter
Smyrna, Georgia

B.C.

SEALPOINT SIAMESE
18-YEAR-OLD MALE
APRIL 1980 - DECEMBER 1998

Dear B.C.,

It's been over a year since you were put down, and I still miss you terribly. I am sitting here trying not to cry, listening to our song. "I'll Be Missing You" by Puff Daddy. The words mean so much to me.

We were a team for my whole life. I remember how you used to call my name when you were sick and how you were always there for me when I was sick. I didn't get to say good bye to you, and that hurts a lot. I remember I came home from school and you weren't there. I called mom, and she just cried. I knew right then what had happened. I had seen your body shutting down for weeks. I told her I was fine and hung up and just cried forever.

I tried not to let people see me cry, but it was hard. Really hard. I remember the night I sat on the living room floor and just cried for hours. I couldn't stop. I used to ask God that this was just a dream...that you would walk down the hall and come into my room. I'd call out to you and expect to see you, but you never came back.

I think of you lying in the box wrapped up in Chris's and my baby blankets, with our pictures so you'll never forget us. I remember eating across from the vet's office the day before you were going to be put to sleep. You were in there probably crying. I wanted to just go get you and hold you, but I couldn't.

I know how selfish I am wanting you back so badly. I'm looking at the picture of us when I was just a baby. I had you all my life, all my life. You were the sweetest most laid-back cat with the sharpest teeth. Ha Ha. You rarely bit unless we were playing.

I take back everything I ever said to you when I was mad or upset.

I take everything back. You were the best and always will be!! Please don't ever think that Sugar is here to replace you 'cause, B.C., no one could EVER replace you, EVER!!!!

I love you, and I'm sorry and one more thing I never got to say to you ... goodbye big brother ...

Love, your little sis for life and beyond,
Loni

Loni Owens
Student, age 14
Battle Creek, Michigan

The smallest feline is a masterpiece.

—Leonardo da Vinci

BABY GIRL

BLACK SHORTHAIR CAT
11-MONTH-OLD FEMALE
JUNE, 1998 - MAY 24, 1999

Dearest Baby Girl,

You came into my life in December, sticking your little paw out of the cage at the shelter, saying take me, take me. I did, along with two others, but you were my heart.

How you sneezed and coughed, and I kept running you to the vet. They would put you on antibiotic after antibiotic. How you hated that, but you would always give in and take your medicine.

You taught me so much, my little dear. How to laugh and how to love again. You brought me such joy and happiness. You would give the other two a run for their lives, how you would throw newspaper and banana peels on their heads. You kept getting sick though, and finally the vet did blood work and, yes, after saying you were free of leukemia...they told me you had the dreaded disease, and I knew you had to leave me.

I held you in my arms and you put your little nose on mine, and then you kissed me and I held you tight and wept and wept. Off to sleep you went...leaving me.

And I thank you my little love for all you gave to me in our short time together. Maybe my punctuation and spelling might be off, but my love for you goes on forever. Wait for me, Baby Girl.

Love, Your Mom,
Pat

Pat Vogel
Retired Licensed Practical Nurse
Pittsburgh, Pennsylvania

BEAR

DOMESTIC SHORTHAIR CAT
2-YEAR-OLD MALE
SPRING 1997 - MAY 5, 1999

I knew I had to stay home from work that day. I wasn't sick, but something wasn't quite right. And then the knock on the door. A voice in my head said, "Ignore it. Whoever it is will go away." But the knocks kept coming. I got up slowly. The young man at the door asked, "Do you have a black cat? It's in the street."

Bear, I don't remember what happened after that. I was at the door, and then I was in the street standing over your body. I can see you there like it is happening again. I looked at your body and knew...you were gone. The spark, the force. Gone.

Just about an hour earlier, you had brought in a grasshopper. I laughed as I took it away. One of your catches; you were the mighty hunter. The day before it had been a large leaf. How many toys did you take from our neighbors? Your favorite toy, I can't look at. Sometimes, Bear, I swear you are dragging that lobster beanie baby with the bell I tied to it jingling behind you. For an instance, my heart leaps. "Bear! Come on buddy! I'll play with you!" Then, remembrance. You're not there.

Everyone tells me, "He had a good life." Thinking about how good your life was doesn't make the pain any less. I love you so much, Bear. Life without you is so strange. But time will pass, and my life will change. But know this Bear, I will never, never forget you. You are a part of me always. One day, Bear, after all the lessons are learned in this life, I will join you again. I have to believe this, because as much as I hurt without you now, the thought of eternity without you is intolerable.

I love you, Bear. You are my good boy. I'll see you soon, buddy.

Colleen Elersich
Customer Service/Administrative Assistant
Simi Valley, California

BELIAL

DOMESTIC LONGHAIR CAT
13-YEAR-OLD MALE
JANUARY 1, 1980 - MARCH 26, 1993

Dear Lolly,

I'm writing to you, sweet Lollipop, because you were the first one I had to let go of as an adult.

It was so hard to let Dr. Tom put you to sleep. When we left for the office that afternoon I still hoped Dr. Tom had at least one more trick up his sleeve.

I'll always remember our cuddling together, how you could knead on my belly for hours. You were the sweetest little soul. I still miss you. The house is still full of kitties, but how many times do I find myself calling you?

It never gets any easier to say good bye, but I'm so glad we took that final visit together. You helped me grow up sweetheart, and none of my kids will ever have to make that trip alone.

I'll always love you,
Mommy

Arlene Domkowski
Professional Pet Sitter
Bridgeport, Connecticut

*I believe cats to be spirits come to earth.
A cat, I'm sure, could walk on a cloud without
coming through.*

—Jules Verne

DOOBERS

TABBY CAT
19-YEAR-OLD MALE
1979 - OCTOBER 9, 1998

One-of-a-Kind Doobers,
    You were always there with a purr and a smile.
    We went through so much together, mile after mile.
    Whenever I saw you, you meowed just like a tiger.
    You lived a good life, but your time has expired.
    You loved sitting behind me in my chair by the computer.
    Now that spot will be empty,
    so long,
    my poor Doobers.
    You loved waiting for me to come home and see you,
    But now you've gone away, and I'm so going to miss you.
    You lived a long life, so full and endearing,
    But when I come home now, there will be just a sad empty feeling.
    You've gone to a better place now,
    Where all God's creatures go.
    There are birds and flowers there,
    But how I'll miss you so.

Lyndon Spear
Stock Trader
Hollywood, Florida

EBONY

BLACK CAT
6-YEAR-OLD FEMALE
UNKNOWN - NOVEMBER 13,1998

You were just a little fur ball when I first saw you in that box, as black as the night itself. Little did I know at that time that you would become my closest friend. We went through all of your litters together. What a great mom you were.

You always seemed to know how I was feeling, whether it be sick or maybe just sad. You always came to be by my side, always there with a nuzzle, a lick and purrrrr that was unforgettable.

I tried to do the best for you today my friend. The doctors said that with the leukemia there is no guarantee that you would get well. The cat on that table was not you. There was no twinkle in your eyes, no purr, just a motionless body.

I will miss you my buddy. I will miss you by my side watching TV, we did that so well together. I will miss our morning coffee.

You will always be in my heart, always by my side...till we meet at the Rainbow Bridge.

Rosanne and Kids

Rosanne Rodriguez
Secretary
Brentwood, New York

JAIDA

TORTOISESHELL CAT
10-YEAR-OLD FEMALE
JANUARY 1985 - SEPTEMBER 19, 1995

Dear Jaida,

When I stop at the mailbox at the end of the driveway after work, I still look toward the house, expecting to see you. Around the corner, you'd come running to meet me; my little black cat. As with most strays, there's usually the question of "who found who," but I remember the day we met.

It sounded more like a bird's chirp than a cat's meow, but when I looked up in the tree, it was a black cat who stared back at me with the biggest, yellowest eyes I'd ever seen. It was obvious you were homeless, and as you stared down at me with those round, sunken, haunted eyes, my heart reached out to you.

I stood on a garbage can and held up a small bowl of cat food. I talked to you for the next 30 minutes while you picked your way slowly down through the branches, squeaking intermittently, hunger winning over distrust.

Remember your first visit to the veterinarian? You saw it from the inside of a big brown towel. It was the only way you would allow yourself to be carried. The marks you'd left on my arms were not your basic "Oh-I-see-you-have-a-new-kitten" caliber of scratches. But I know you were just frightened.

Almost fourteen years have passed since then, including the four that you've been gone. I still think of you, Jaida. I haven't forgotten how you'd always travel to the vet wrapped in a towel — your terrycloth cocoon; how you'd curl up on the table with your head buried under your paws, and you'd purr in attempt to comfort yourself. We made plenty of doctor visits over the years because your health was never really 100 percent. Thank you for trusting me and for knowing that I was trying to help you.

You had a rough time at the end. We both did. I wanted so much to do what was best for you. Sometimes it's hard to accept that letting go is the kindest act of love. I stayed up with you that last night, bathing you in warm water and cuddling you in front of the heater. When I felt you slipping away, I begged you to stay with me, and you did. You held on at the vet's throughout the next day, too. They didn't know how you were able to find that strength. But I knew. I knew you.

Jaida, thank you for waiting for me to return to the vet's that afternoon. Thank you for letting me be with you and hold you and talk to you one last time before you had to go. You spared me from having to make that decision for you, because you went on your own. I don't know if I could have made a conscious decision to let you go. I don't think I had it in me at the time. You knew that, didn't you. You went into convulsions in my arms and they rushed you in the operatory, but it was too late. I knelt down next to the table and held your head in my hands, your face covered with an oxygen mask. I could barely see you through my tears. Did you hear me say good-bye? Did you know I was there with you at your last moment, telling you that I was sorry?

You'll always be special to me. Every time you sought out my lap to sit in or rubbed against my leg, I could feel your trust, and it meant a lot because I know you didn't trust easily. You made me feel special, too.

When I think of you, Jaida, the image of that sick, emaciated, frightened cat fades in my memory, and all I see is my little friend rounding the corner, running down the driveway toward me as I stand at the mailbox. Thank you. We'll be together again one day, and you can sit in my lap forever.

Love,
Laura

I had no reason to believe
that I wouldn't continue to live the solitary life that I was
accustomed to, but one day this little animal walked in from
nowhere as though she had been invited and my whole
existence has changed.

—James Herriot

KIKI ANN SANDRA STEWART

DOMESTIC LONGHAIR CAT, TABBY & WHITE
22-YEAR-OLD FEMALE
JULY 5, 1977 - JUNE 30, 1999

To My Dearest Kiki,

Although it has only been a month since I last looked into your beautiful copper eyes it feels like an eternity. I can't begin to tell you what I am going through because there are no words to describe it. I would give ANYTHING to hold you once again and tell you what an important part of my life you are. You were with me through everything from the time I was ten months old.

Renal failure not only took your life, it took mine as well. Home doesn't feel like home without you here. I am so sorry that it had to come down to me having to put you down. It was the hardest decision I have ever or will ever have to make in my whole life. I have so many selfish regrets for not staying with you while the vet put you at "comfort," knowing that you had to go to the Bridge on your own with a bunch of strangers standing around you at the vet's. Baby, if I could turn back time I would, you know that! I am so sorry Kook!

Waiting to see the vet. That day felt like I was waiting forever, and when he told me to put you to sleep that day, it felt like my heart dropped to my ankles. I'm sorry, Honey, but Mommy couldn't do it without trying everything possible first. That is why I put you on an I.V. that night, and I prayed with everything in me for God not to take you from me, your time here wasn't done yet. And when I got that call in the morning to come in to sign papers to have you euthanised because there was nothing that they could do for you, I wanted to die myself.

To see you in so much pain was so hard for me when I went to say good-bye. When I think of you and all the great times we shared together, it makes me want to smile and be thankful that I had such a great baby in my life, but all I can do is cry.

But, remember what I told you, "Forever In Our Heart, We'll Never Be Apart." Mommy meant every word of it! And remember, too, that when I do get another cat to keep Tunsis company (her best is now gone) that no matter what, no one could ever, ever take the place that you still hold in my heart. Thinking of you being twenty-two when you left makes it a little easier. Also, knowing that you had an amazing life with unconditional love helps my grieving some, but not enough. Even writing to you EACH day in a journal and lighting a spiritual candle helps a little.

I really miss you "nesting" in my hair each night and sharing a pillow with me, but looking at the cat dishes and not seeing you there really hurts me. You are the best gift that could ever be given, but now they took you back. I wish I knew how you are doing. If you're happy, or depressed and lonely like me. Some day, my Angel, we will meet again, and like I asked you, please be the first one to greet me and there I will kiss and hold you in my arms...but this time FOREVER! I promise.

Until we meet again my Angel, I will hold your ashes forever close to my heart.

Love And Miss You Like Crazy, Mamma Bear!!!

Forever,
Mommy
XO XO XO XO

Nancy Stewart
Homemaker
Wawa, Ontario, Canada

KITTY

LONGHAIR TORTOISESHELL CAT
15-YEAR-OLD FEMALE
JUNE 24, 1984 - AUGUST 1, 1999

My Dearest Kitty-Angel-Princess,

Just two days ago our lives have forever changed. We found out that no matter how much we love you or wish for it, you cannot stay with us any longer. It is your time to move on to eternity without us. I wish that our love will carry you to a place in which the sunbeams shine on you all day and warm your silky hair, and where you are served platters of tuna, chicken and turkey.

Since we brought you back home and were told to just make you comfortable, I'm so worried that you are in pain. As much as I want to hold on to you here and now, I am so afraid that you could hurt. But how do I pick the day for you to die? I want every minute of every day with you, but I also want you to go in peace before you feel pain. How do I choose? Which day will it be? What if I wait too long, or what if I had waited another day and a miracle could have happened? How do I know what you want? I am so afraid of being selfish and letting you live longer than you want to, just to have some more time with you, because I cannot imagine a day without you.

Now I look at you and try to drink in all your features. You are so delicate and graceful, your long arms, legs and neck, your silky, fluffy hair, always well groomed. You always appeared dainty, almost fragile — except for your spirit. You have to be strong to go the rest of the way alone. I'm so sorry that Mommy can't be with you, but I hope that one day we will be reunited and then be together for all eternity. I hope that YinYang will be with you and show you the way.

I thank you for your love and companionship, every knead on my belly and legs, every lick at my hands, even every nip at my feet! You have loved me unconditionally, and you have taught me to be more tolerant and patient, more forgiving and tender. You would comfort me when I was sad or hurt, and amuse me when I needed to laugh. Many people didn't understand my love for you, me treating you like my child, but in a way you are and always will be. I could not possibly love a child any more than I love you.

My life will never be the same without you. I already miss you so very, very much. I will be without my Little-Kitty-Girl who has given me so much joy. I will miss running my hands over your hair, once brown and black, now mixed with silvery gray. Stroking your hair often made me feel calm, connected with you, my sweet little girl.

I'll miss your happy chatter. Our home will be silent of your unique language. How I now wish I had taped your sweet voice. And your eyes...as a kitten the brightest blue, and for years now a gorgeous green with sparks of light in them — I will always remember the love I see within them. You are my precious "Little-Kitty-Girl," my angel. Watch over me and feel how much I will always love you. I will miss you greeting me at the door whenever I come home — you always make me feel so special.

I sit here, with a little candle burning in your honor, and you just sat down at my feet. You are so very tiny now, and yet your spirit fills the room. You never asked for much, but enjoyed all we were able to give you. I am grateful that I am able to remain with you most of the time now, hopefully making your transition easier.

Death as a concept and a reality scares me so much, I just hope that I'm not transmitting any negative feelings to you. I have not been able to stop crying since you became ill. In my heart I knew that you were nearing your end. I understand your life span simply was always destined to be shorter, but that just doesn't make losing you any easier. I grieve for you already, and you are still with me. But you have already changed. In subtle ways you are already preparing yourself for your final journey, suddenly shrinking from my touch, separating yourself from this life. All I want to do is pick you up and hug you and love you and hold you tight. All I want to do is hold on to you, but I know that I cannot.

I sit here crying and crying and don't seem able to stop. I catch you watching me sometimes, and I don't mean to upset you, but I can't imagine you not being in my life. You have been with me my entire adult life, seeing me through happy times, sad times, illness, lack of money, comfort and contentment.

I am afraid to end this letter, afraid that when I stop, you will end being. I thank the universe for our time together. It seems much too short. Time has moved quickly and life just seemed to happen along the way. There is so much I still want to tell you, things that I am just too sad to think of right now. I fear that some memories will fade and I don't want them to — I don't want to forget anything about you. I feel blessed to have been graced with your love and companionship. I thank you for allowing me to take care of you. You are the greatest gift I ever could have been given.

I don't know where you're going. I'm sorry that you must go the rest of the path alone. Don't be afraid. I will miss you so desperately, but my heart is filled with my love for you. I want so much to believe that we will be reunited again when I die, but I just don't know what to believe about death and where we all go. I want so much to see you again, this just can't be all there is. Visit me in my dreams. Remember and feel my love. Be safe my friend. Good-bye for now.

All my love,
Mommy

Nina Ruch
Metaphysical Gift Shop Owner
Tacoma, Washington

I love cats because I enjoy my home;
and little by little they become its visible soul.

—Jean Cocteau

LEROY MCNABB

TIGER-STRIPED TABBY
6-MONTH-OLD MALE
SEPTEMBER 28, 1998 - MARCH 30, 1999

My Sweet Little Guy,

I miss you so much. I still can't believe that you are gone. I feel like a part of my soul has been taken away. The spot on my pillow where you used to sleep seems so bare without you there with me. It has been over a month now since you had to leave this world, but I still miss you so much. I have saved all of your little toys for you, and I still make a spot for you to sleep with me at night.

I can never forgive myself for having to decide to have you put to sleep. I know that your little heart was sick and that you were suffering, but I know that you were holding on for me. I know that you didn't show me earlier that something was wrong because you didn't want me to worry.

I miss you so much my little sweets. You were just a baby, it doesn't seem fair. You were so special to me and still are. I will never forget you or try to replace you because I can't. You were my little shadow, you followed me everywhere. You always purred when you were with me...always. Sometimes it was so loud that I couldn't sleep, but I didn't care. You were my little guy, my precious little fur. I miss you so much. I miss how you used to lick me in the face, how you would chase me around, how you followed me everywhere, and how you ran to meet me when I got home with your little mews and your funny meow. I remember when I brought you home that rainy night. You played with me in the car the entire time.

I miss you so much. You are such a part of me and always will be. Here on Earth, your little heart loved me so much that it couldn't take it...it just got too big for your tiny body. But in Heaven, you can continue to love me all you want without worrying about limits to what your little body can do. One day we will be together again and we can play and run and jump and chase each other all we want. Without getting tired, or sick, or separated again.

I am so sorry that I couldn't do more to help you. I was there holding you when you took your last breath, and I felt your little heart stop beating. That was the most that I could do for you. I didn't want you to be with strangers. I wanted you to know up to the last minute how much I love you and how sorry I am that I couldn't do anything to make you better. I can still feel your little heart stop beating. That was the most precious thing that we could have ever shared. I love you my little guy, I will love you forever. Please don't hate me for what I had to do. I love you so much and you were suffering.

Had I known that you had this heart problem when I got you, it would not have changed my mind about bringing you home with me. I was so honored to have the five-and-a-half months with you that I did. I would not change that for anything in the world. I would rather have had those five-and-a-half months with you in my life than no time at all. I have memories of you now, and I still feel you in my heart and that was worth everything that has happened.

I miss you so much, but I know that you are waiting for me in Heaven. I know that you are in Heaven because only God could create such a being capable of the love that you showed me. And if you were really the gift from God that I believe that you are, then I don't see why He would not take you back. I know that you are waiting for me...I know it. You would have been seven months old just a few days ago. I miss you so much my special little guy.

You came into my life and gave me such wonderful memories and funny stories to share. You loved me and still do, I believe, so unconditionally that I know that you are a gift from God. Everyday I thank Him for letting me know you and for letting me be there to hold you when you took your last breath. I love you, I love you my special little guy. Those were the last words you heard me speak.

You are in Heaven now with my other kitty, Murry, and he is taking such good care of you...I know he is. He was special just like you. You guys were so much alike that it is uncanny. Stay with Murry and play with him until I can be with you both again. I promise that we will have eternity together to play and sleep and purr and chase each other. I miss you guys so much. Keep each other company and remember how much I love you both. You are my special men, my little gifts from God. You both touched my life so profoundly that I could never stop loving you or ever forget about you.

I still keep a place in my bed open for where you liked to sleep, just in case you want to stop in and sleep with me some night. Sometimes I feel like you are here with me. Please forgive me and know this...I love you both very much and you will always be a part of me. Good-bye for now my little guys, take care of each other and wait for me. You both have souls that shine more brightly than any star ever could. I will find you one day...I promise, and it will be a wonderful reunion.

With all of the love that I could ever have hoped for from you both,
Your Jenny-Jenny

Jennifer Warner
Graduate Student
Pittsburgh, Pennsylvania

LUISA

SASSY FARM CAT
19-YEAR-OLD FEMALE
JULY 24, 1982 - JULY 20, 1999

Where to begin? Tomorrow will be the last day you wake up, meow your strange deaf-cat sounds, curl up into your fuzzy white self on the laundry so that we can't tell what's what, lick someone's finger six hundred times, chase some stray sunbeam's reflection off a watch, sip from the tap in the bathroom upstairs, miss the box when you're taking a leak, climb up Dad's pants and shirt to sit on his shoulder, chase invisible things around the backyard, only half way up the tree cuz yer getting old, hook your paw in the vet's chin and grrr at yourself in the mirror, chase a flashlight's beam around the house while I chase you with my video camera, get your head stuck in a pitcher of water trying to drink it, drag home a fat green worm who's goo drips down your chin, perch like a pharaoh on the log stump outside and rest like a sphinx in the sunbeam on the arm of the couch. Luisa, dba ZI. Doing business as ZI!

How I love and respect you, how much I appreciate having shared my life with you. How sad I am to be far away from you for these last two years, knowing that you feel abandoned but don't understand why. Life, youth to adulthood and more: we did this together. You joined my life when I was eight, the only deaf, one-blue, one-green eyed cat I've ever known. You have shaped me.

I hate growing up. The ones we love die, and then there's just this hole in your soul where there used to be white hairs, noises, messes. I've been ready, since Sylvester died. I clipped some of your cute, fuzzy, curly belly hair.

I'm working, and I'm so busy, and so far away from you. I forget sometimes, and when I remember I feel sick. Sometimes I think it's okay, I can let go: you're so old, and need rest. But you're my baby, so beautiful, and such a grouchy old lady — I have these memories to keep you alive — I will dream about you. Then I think of the house, my life without you. Think about growing old. I feel really torn.

I love you and want you to know this. My love is complex: is it right to remove an animal from its community and impose another social structure? Did you feel like a part of our family? Did I do right by you? How will your last moments be? Will you die knowing that we love you? Will you have peace?

I want to be the one who dresses you, puts sweet things in your box, wraps you in my favorite clothes — kisses you one last time. There is so much to say and show that cannot be. It is all inside me, unspeakable. I want to make your memory meaningful. I want people to remember you, even though they did not know you. I want everyone to know you.

This brings out sorrow in Mom and Dad, who are now even more anxious without us there, thinking this could happen to them anytime. I can't deal with it. It's too much guilt. Zi, I love you. I will always love you. I will also release you — release you into the next life. I will sing for you.

This is a two day letter. Now it's the next day, and it's happened, and Mom says you're in your usual ball, on the couch, waiting for her to put sweet things in your box. I feel your spirit around me and I'm so happy, but I also can't stop crying.

I don't need to say good-bye. This is a new kind of hello. Luisa, I love you, I'll always be with you.

Rosanna D'Agnillo
Musician
San Francisco, California

Who can believe that there is no soul
behind those luminous eyes!

—Theophile Gautier

LUKE SKYWALKER

DOMESTIC SHORTHAIR CAT
10- OR 11-YEAR-OLD MALE
UNKNOWN - APRIL 23, 1999

Dear Luke,

I miss you. We all miss you. Max and Jane are looking for you. I remember how they comforted you when your legs buckled and you lay paralysed on the floor. I want you to know that you were not being punished for anything. You were always a wonderful cat.

I am so sorry that your death had to be so labourous and painful. Even after the lethal injection by the vet, your heart refused to stop beating, and you struggled to breathe. Did you think that I needed your love? Is that why you refused to die?

In my mind, I do not see you romping over fields or chasing mice, instead, you are in front of a continuously refilled food bowl, next to a sunbeam, ready to roll over on your back and sleep so peacefully.

I hope you are at peace now, Luke. I know that my tears cannot bring you back, but still I am crying. You weren't there this morning to wake me up — I slept in for the first time since I brought you home. I miss you, Luke.

I will never forget you,
Virginia

P.S: Please, today as you go about your lives, do as Luke did, and be kind to people, dogs and cats.

Virginia Parker
Teacher
La Pocatiere, Quebec, Canada

MEESH

AMERICAN SHORTHAIR CAT
6½-YEAR-OLD FEMALE
NOVEMBER 10, 1992 - JUNE 21, 1999

Dear Meesh,

It is so hard to say good-bye to my beautiful white cat with the sky blue eyes. You truly lightened up my days since you first arrived at our house.

I remember the day that we received a call from the Humane Society. The lady there said that she had this beautiful white cat with big blue eyes. She said that your fur was as white as a cloud and soft like a rabbit's. She thought you would be a perfect cat to join our other white cat, K.C. I left immediately for the Humane Society to meet you. It was love at first sight. I was looking for a "cuddle cat" and you fit the description.

You were already three years old when you arrived at our home. I enjoyed the way that you greeted me when I came home from teaching school. You would go to the kitchen and lie down and want your stomach rubbed. If I did not do this, you would meow and meow until I gave in. Oh that meow! It was your sign for everything. If you wanted food you meowed. If you wanted a toy you meowed, and if you just wanted attention you meowed. Oh, how I miss the meowing now that you are gone.

Three short years was all that we were given with you. You became my companion. When I was very sick last summer, you spent the days lying cuddled next to me in bed. It was your purring that comforted me when I was in such pain. You sustained me with your devotion. Now there is an empty place next to me and an emptiness in my heart.

I don't understand why you were taken from me. I apologize for not seeing the signs of the illness that you had. I did see your body becoming weaker, and that is when I took you to the veterinarian.

We discovered that you had a fever, and we thought it was caused by the abscess that you had on your neck. You were given antibiotics and I thought you would be fine in a few days. Instead you got weaker and weaker and would not eat. You became a mere image of the beautiful cat that I had brought home three years earlier. You were not able to walk or even meow like normal.

We drove to the veterinary hospital at Michigan State with hope in my heart that they would be able to find out what was wrong with you. When the doctor said that she needed to do tests on you and that you would need to stay at the hospital, I kissed you good-bye. Little did I know it would be the last time I would be able to touch that rabbit-soft fur and hear your beautiful purr.

The veterinarian called later that night and said that you had cancer of the blood and something about the cancer being in your bone marrow and that it was robbing you of oxygen and shutting down your vital organs. The word "terminal" broke my heart. I knew what I had to do, but it was so difficult to say the words. Six-and-a-half years old is too young to die. I kept remembering your beautiful blue eyes and all of the wonderful times that we spent together. I hope you understand why I had you put to sleep. I just couldn't let you suffer. I loved you enough to say good-bye. Until we meet again Meesh, I will always keep your memory close to my heart.

Good-bye for now,
Nancy, Terry, K.C. and Smudgie

Nancy Willyard
Elementary School Teacher
Jackson, Michigan

MITSY

BLACK & WHITE CAT
3-YEAR-OLD FEMALE
1994 - FEBRUARY 1997

Dear Mitsy,

Four years ago when we found you, you were just a small black and white kitten living in a shopping center parking lot. Daddy and I had always been dog people, but we bought you a can of food and waited while you got up the courage to come and eat it. As I watched you eating, something came over me and I just knew I had to take you home with me.

It was like you had lived with us all your little life. You never once hid or seemed nervous, and you bonded so very closely to Mommy. I know that I was the only one you wanted to touch you other than Daddy, occasionally. It should have been our happy ending to a sad start.

Then we had to go to the kitty doctor for a check-up. You tested positive for kitty leukemia. The doctor told us that many kitties live pretty long lives and sometimes even test negative on a second or third blood test. We prayed for that. For three years Mommy refused to have you re-tested. Maybe I was afraid of what would hear, and I so wanted to keep our attitudes positive. Besides, I was sure the first test was wrong, you were not sick, you were healthy and happy and smart, too. We would fool them all.

I loved how you curled by my neck every night purring away, and never missed an opportunity to jump on my lap, make bread on my shoulders, and push my glasses off my eyes so you could look at me. You loved to chase those silver-paper balls and bring them back to me again and again. I loved butting foreheads with you from the kitchen counter, as you watched me wash dishes or cook. I never dreamed I would love you this much.

When you started breathing funny that Sunday morning I thought it was just a cold, but Daddy and I rushed you to the special kitty doctor anyway. I didn't know you were so sick. You never gave me the slightest clue until that morning. The doctor examined you. Your lungs and stomach were filled with fluid, and so he insisted on the dreaded test. You know how that turned out. They took you away from me that morning, and life has never been quite the same since.

I have adopted two new kittens to help fill the hole you left in my heart. Besides, I figured that your mission in your little life was to make some mushy cat-person out of me, so I do not want to let you down. Anyway, your new brother and sister, Smoky and Bandit, both tested negative to everything, and they will hopefully be with Daddy and me for many years to come.

But I just had to say thank you Mitsy, my precious little black and white angel. I will never forget you, I promise.

Until we all meet again,
Love, Mommy

Patricia Davis
Paralegal
Miami, Florida

All animals, except man, know that
the principal business of life is to enjoy it.

—Samuel Butler

MONGO

DOMESTIC CAT
10-YEAR-OLD MALE
APRIL 15, 1989 - JUNE 1999

Mongo,

My sweet little man. I used to call you a lot of nicknames and you would always come to what ever it was I called you. You somehow knew that it was you I was talking to. You blessed our lives for ten years with your love and kisses. You always knew how to make me smile when I was down. You accepted all of the changes that came over the ten years that you were with us. I know that some of these changes you did not like, but you still accepted them because you loved us.

Well, my sweet child, we loved you so much in return, and I know that you knew that. I regret the day of your passing and I always will. I could not save you, my baby. If I could turn back time, you would still be here with me, and my heart would not be so sad.

I will miss you and I will never forget you, my baby. I know you are at the Bridge waiting for me, and I know Cinders and Ashley and Baby are there with you as well. I know you are healthy and happy there waiting for me. We will be together again someday. I love and miss you all.

Always remembered, always loved,
Mom & Dad
Poohbear - Kitty sister
P.B. Max - ferret brother
Sammy - ferret brother

Sue Hamidy
Homemaker
Greeneville, Tennessee

POOKIE

TABBY CAT
15-YEAR-OLD FEMALE
MAY 1984 - JUNE 17, 1999

My Dearest Pookie,

I'm so sorry I had to make the decision I did today. I hope you know I made it out of love. If I knew how much I would be hurting right now, I don't know if I would have made the same decision. I hope I would have, for your sake.

I miss you so much, baby. You're the only one I have ever said, "I love you" to and really meant it. We had fifteen beautiful years together. I'm sorry for all the times I yelled at you for doing stupid things (but they really were stupid things) and thank you for always forgiving me. I guess that's what unconditional love is. Thank you for always being there for me.

I hope you're happy now, punkin. That's why I made the decision today. You weren't happy anymore, not being able to walk, not being able to eat (and I know how much you loved to eat.) I had some cherry ice cream tonight, but it wasn't as good without you bothering me for a taste. I wish you were here right now to share my ice cream. I'd let you have the whole thing just to see your precious face again.

I miss you sweetie pie, fuzzy face. I dread sleeping alone tonight. It hurts so much. I know I'll stop crying eventually. Don't think that means I don't love you anymore. It just means I'm remembering more of the good times than the bad. My darling, Pookie, Mommy loves you FOREVER.

Ginny Renta
Word Processing
Schaumburg, Illinois

SIMBA

TABBY CAT
2½-YEAR-OLD MALE
AUGUST, 1996 - JANUARY 25, 1999

Tribute To Simba:

How do I ever begin to describe you and how you touched my life? You were found in a parking lot on Friday, September 13, 1996. No superstitions here!

You were aggressive and ornery. By that I mean delightful and devilish. When it was feeding time, you would push Sebastian away and eat from his dish. He willingly gave in.

When something spooked you as it sometimes did, you would arch your back and jump sideways, as if to say, "Hey, I'm bad." How I will miss seeing you sleeping in front of the radiator in the bathroom, and with Sam on her bed. You and Sebastian romping around the floor, then both running off in opposite directions. I miss you jumping up on my lap and purring so loud. Gosh, how I miss you and your purring.

When you got lost those six long weeks, we thought we'd never see you again. I was worried and looked for you all the time. You were found, but in such a sad way. You were just barely alive. We got you to the animal hospital, and with love and good care we thought you would bounce back to the once healthy little guy you used to be. But you did not bounce back. You were there for two days in an incubator and on I.V's, and then we brought you home for that last weekend ever. We gave you so much love and affection. You slept with Sam that night. The next day you cuddled with me on the sofa to watch T.V.

That same evening we saw how bad you felt, you were declining fast, my little love. We had to take you back very late that night to the animal hospital, for that last good-bye. We were with you till the very end as you drew your final breath, and my heart felt like it was being ripped out when the vet said the words, "He's gone." I never thought my heart could ache so bad. At least now you were warm and loved, not dying out on some cold street. God gave you back to us for our last reunion and our last good-bye.

I miss you my little friend, and my heart still aches for you! If ever a person met you that did not like cats, they would feel differently after you. You were truly a blessing, unique and exceptional. I will always love you, and someday we will meet again at Rainbow Bridge, never again to be separated ... 'til then, be happy, Sweet Simba.

Always in my heart,
Love, Mom,
Riesa

Riesa Graham-Larson
Lab Technician
New Castle, Delaware

Perhaps one reason why we are fascinated by cats
is because such a small animal can contain so much
independence, dignity, and freedom of spirit.
The cat demands acceptance on his own terms
as the wildest of tame animals
and the tamest of wild ones.

—Lloyd Alexander

SMOKIE

RUSSIAN BLUE CAT
3-YEAR-OLD MALE
1993 - JULY 3, 1996

My Dear Smokie,

You were oh, so much more than a pet...you were my best friend. You stuck by me when my husband and I were separated; you were always there for me no matter what. You were my pillow for my tears at night in bed. You never flinched when one teardrop fell on your silky coat. You were an angel in disguise. My dear Smokie, you left me on July 3, 1996. You loved to go outside and sit in the front yard and bat at the butterflies in the tall grass. This is what cost you your life. Our neighbor next door saw you outside and because they didn't like cats, they let their dog out of the house and it attacked and killed you, my beloved friend. It's been many years now since you've been gone, but tears still come to my eyes writing this. I will never forget you; you will never leave my heart.

Why people are so cruel when they know how special animals can be in their lives, I will never know. I ask people in your name, Smokie, please don't be cruel, and if you see abuse, please report it.

Paula

Paula Howard
Bakery Worker
Ringgold, Georgia

SNUGGLES

DOMESTIC CAT
14-YEAR-OLD FEMALE
SEPTEMBER 1985 - OCTOBER 10, 1999

I took you in and you slept on the side of my neck, hence your name, Snuggles. I could not have asked for a better cat. I adopted five more cats, and you were very patient with them. They knew you ruled the household.

I miss you lying in front of the computer when I tried to write or play games. How I wish you were here now, doing the same thing. You tolerated numerous moving experiences with me without qualms. It was more like, "Here we go again!"

You started to ail the most, I will remember, on that Friday before you had to be put to sleep. You went to the park driveway and caught your last grasshopper. That was your favorite pastime of all. I miss you very much. I still don't know how to tell you good-bye.

Love,
Mom

Connie M. Bejger
Material Handler
Garrettsville, Ohio

TABATHA ANNE ELIZABETH "TABBY"

CAT
15-YEAR-OLD FEMALE
JANUARY 8, 1984 - APRIL 17, 1999

Dear Tabby,

Although you've only been gone a little over a month now, it feels like forever. I miss you so much and think of you every single day. My tears don't fall as often as they did in the beginning, but the hole in my heart is still there...I think it always will be. I really believe part of me died when you left. Although things have gotten a little easier for Mommy, life is strangely different since you have been gone. It just doesn't feel the same in my world anymore ... I miss you so much.

I created a "special" place for you in our apartment. I have a beautiful picture of you in a cherrywood frame, a crystal cat candle, and your ashes in a rose tin. Every Monday, Mommy lights the cat candle for you. God, I am missing you so much right now ... I'm crying as I write you this letter. I wish you were here with me, rubbing against my leg so that I would pick you up. I wish I could hold you again. I wish that you never had to die and that you, your brother Sam, and I were a happy family again. There is a little happiness in our home again though. You'll be glad to hear that Sam is eating again and isn't as depressed. Actually he's been quite angry lately. I guess its because of the new kitten.

I know that you understand that it was time for a new baby. Mommy's heart has so much love in it, and there was a kitten out there who needed Mommy. I named her Elizabeth...after you. She is adorable, but boy, it's been a long time since Mommy had a kitten in the house! She is pretty much into everything! She likes to sleep in a lot of your special places around the apartment. I believe it's because she has an Angel kitty showing her around! Sam really doesn't care for her too much, but it's going to take some time, I guess. Sam still misses you a lot ... I can see it in his eyes. Mommy misses you too. There isn't a day that goes by that I don't think of you. I can't wait for the day when we can all be together again. Until that day...I only need to close my eyes and open my heart to feel your warm and soft body again in my arms. I miss you, my Tabby.

Love always and forever and ever,
Mommy

Lorra E. Allen
Pittsburgh, Pennsylvania

God made the cat
in order that man might have the pleasure
of caressing the tiger.

—Fernand Mery

THADDEUS OWENS

DOMESTIC LONGHAIR BLACK CAT
4-YEAR-OLD MALE
FEBRUARY 1, 1995-APRIL 23, 1999

Dear Thaddeus,

There is no easy way to begin this letter. There is no easy way to say good-bye to you. Today and every day after, I will think of you and smile. And I'll wish we had more time together.

I remember the first time I saw you. I came home and saw your brother sitting on our bed, and Daddy said, "Look on the window sill. There's another one." I met two bright green eyes that were so incredibly beautiful and intelligent, and I fell in love with both of you. That's the night I met my Boys.

We named you first, Thad. We picked out the name Thaddeus to be different. But you were every inch your name—charming, regal, and beautiful. Your personality abounded and your brother, Persseus, idolized you. You were more adventurous and outgoing and much more vocal. But it was obvious to us that your brother was very important to you. You two were never apart—declawed together, neutered together. And you were the best companions I could have had when Daddy had to work late. You could never have enough attention.

Then came The Struggle. You were so defiant, Thaddie, never wanted to use the cat box or listen. A vet tech told me, "They have to decide who will be the king and who will be the prince." There was no doubt in my mind who would win. You, Thad, were made to be a king.

You were so incredibly vocal. We knew what every one of your cries meant. Frustration, impatience, expectation, and contentment. We always called you the Purr Machine. But your most vocal times were when you were mad! Oh, could you yell at us. Food a little late, we weren't home on time — heaven help us. You would give us looks like, "Who do you think you are? I run this show." And the ultimate rebuff? You would sit with your back to us, look over your shoulder, establish eye contact, then close your eyes and turn away. You knew you did something bad when Thaddie gave you that treatment. But you'd always come around not long after, letting us know all was forgiven. Your personality stills oozes over this apartment.

Then one day when you were two-and-a-half, Mommy and Daddy did the unthinkable. We brought another cat home. It wasn't just The Boyos anymore. Thaddeus and Persseus had a sister.

But Sydney was easy to manage for you. You were still the king, but now you had a queen to go along with your crown prince. After you all stopped hissing, The Girlie (as she's better known) was an instant companion. She loved playing with you. You were so good with her. You let her bite your neck, your back, your ears, your tail...you name it, she bit it. She would pounce on you with her most unimpressive size (she's only nine pounds and you were at one time sixteen). And you, being the charming, loving, big brother that you are, would flop over, oh so melodramatically and let her win. We loved to watch you.

At almost four years old, Thaddie-cakes, you got sick. Your size, your diet, and your gender all worked against you. You were sick a long time and didn't let on. Starting in January of '99, you underwent many procedures to relieve your blockages. In February, after turning four, you had major surgery because your bladder was about to rupture. We nursed you through that awful time and saw the intense pain you were in. Believing a minor surgery would help you, we took you to the vet and wanted to have it done. Instead, they found a growth in your urethra, and there was nothing we could do. We chose not to wake you from the sedation. I couldn't look into those beautiful green eyes and say goodbye. We couldn't let you suffer any more than you had.

Mommy and Daddy stayed with you until the end, Thaddie. Wild horses couldn't have dragged me from your side. We had such little time with you, I wasn't going to let anyone take those final seconds away.

Now I see you on the window sill or perched in your cat tree. Sometimes I hear you eating in the kitchen or running around pouncing on a Q-tip. Persey goes from room to room looking for the brother that has always been there. And The Girlie has stationed herself by the door, waiting for you to walk in.

We miss you, Thaddie, and we don't know what to do. You were the only one who liked to be brushed, the only one who liked to be picked up and carried around. And I miss doing those things. But, if I had to do those things with you in so much pain and suffering so badly, I would rather not do them. In my mind, I know we did the right thing, but my heart hasn't been told yet. I know that if I had to do it all over again with a choice between you and a cat that would always be healthy, I would choose you.

We will take good care of Persey and The Girlie, Sydney. And we are happy you are out of pain. One day far from now, hopefully I will see you again. Until then, Thaddie-boy, I love you with all my heart. Give me kissee, baby. Love you, boyo.

Love, Mommy
and Mike, Persseus, The Girlie-Sydney, Monty

Monica Owens
Embroidery Machine Operator
Oak Creek, Wisconsin

TOAST

DOMESTIC SHORTHAIR CAT, BLACK/BROWN TIGER
8½-YEAR-OLD MALE
NOVEMBER 12, 1990 - MAY 28, 1999

Ah, My Sweet Little Toaster,

This letter is not for you, my big guy. This letter is for me. And although you've been gone for two weeks now, I'm still struggling to accept your death. Maybe this letter will help me. Help me remember your life, not grieve your death. Help me smile when I think of you, not cry.

I think of you all the time. Only a week ago at a restaurant the waitperson asked, "Muffin, toast, or pancakes." My voice broke when I sadly responded, "Toast, please." I'd give anything if having you back were as easy as saying, "Toast, please." But I know that I can't have you back. I stroked your panting side and whispered goodbyes as you died on the kitchen floor; I dug your grave out in the garden in the spot you'd picked out the Monday before you died; I put your little paw over your eyes the way you used to do when sleeping; I wrapped you carefully in your green blanket; and I buried you.

I know I can't have you back. But I can remember. And I will always remember the Little Boy with the too big heart, my Toast. And no, you weren't named for bread. As I frequently told people who asked, "He's the verb, not the noun." You were my New Year's boy coming home on January 8, 1991. Eight weeks old, full of spit and spirit, and covered in fuzzy tiger stripes with those great cream circles outlining your eyes. You were a Toast to new beginnings. A celebration that life does go on. After all, my Punch had died and her surviving daughter, Bagel, needed a companion. So did I.

Even as a little guy you had that big heart and lots of snuggles. You'd curl up next to Bag on the couch and "be good" so she wouldn't swat you. You'd cuddle on the floor with your stuffed bear, often sleeping with your paw over the bear's arm and your little nose pushed under her chin. And you'd crawl up my blue-jeaned leg to find a comfy spot in my arms for afternoon kitty naps. I miss those afternoon naps. I miss you.

Once you'd reached sixteen pounds, cuddling wasn't so comfy, but your big heart still made you the snuggle cat. Morning coffee time found you more comfortable perching on my lap with your paws hugging my shoulders. The head-butts against my chin, the light nips at my nose, and that ever-constant rumble purr made morning-time a special time. I miss those mornings. I miss you.

Sometimes though, your big heart made you the most tolerant cat. Leash training was so easy. We'd walk blocks on warm summer evenings while you stopped to sniff the flowers, eat the neighbor's boulevard grass, and every now and then hold your instincts when bunnies crossed our path. A gentle tug, a whispered, "No, Toast, let's go," was all it took to keep you moving on the right path. I miss those walks. I miss you.

But then in February, the walks stopped; the leash rested unused by the front door; and I worried. Our local vet said it was serious. "Can you take him to the Veterinary Medicine Teaching Hospital in Madison tonight?" Your breathing was labored, and you were so sick. Two hours later in Madison we found out why. Congestive heart failure. After oxygen therapy and an ultrasound, the diagnosis broke my heart. For the little boy who'd always had so much heart had idiopathic hypertrophic cardiomyopathy, a too big heart. You were only eight. I cried.

I cried when your health returned and you sat up and begged by the front door. We had a few more walks. I cried when you returned to the bed to nuzzle and nip my ears. We had a few more snuggle nights with you snoring at the foot of the bed. I cried when you again sat on the floor near my computer desk chair with your quiet mew asking permission to jump into my lap. We play fought over the mouse a few more times. But I knew the path you were on was a short one. And no matter how much I'd gently tug, no matter how much I'd whisper, "No, Toast," I knew you soon would leave. And then you did.

I said goodbye so many times those last three months. You did, too. But it wasn't enough. I miss you so much. I'm crying now, but I'm also smiling ... smiling not for what I've lost; I'm smiling for what I had. I had Toast, the little boy with the too big heart.

Forever, big guy, you have my heart. Thank you for giving so much. And thank you for leaving all the memories. They will get me through. It will be a long path, I know. But I feel you gently tugging, and I hear you softly whispering, "No, Marilyn, let's go."

Love,
Marilyn

Marilyn Schiel
Teacher
Stevens Point, Wisconsin

ZEPHY

SIAMESE MIX
16-YEAR-OLD MALE
JULY 10, 1983 - JUNE 13, 1999

My Beloved Zephy,

It has been three days since your vicious death by a pitbull in the neighborhood. I remember you looking around that morn and then up at me. And I said what I always did, "Okay, you're outside now. You be safe, okay?" An hour later you were dead. To find your still body ripped my soul. I pray you went fast and left not with the fear and pain of your last moments, but with all the love I shared with you. As well as all the love you both gave and received from all who knew you. Some of my clients asked if you could come in the room during treatment and you always added your kitty healing to so many. Zephy you were walking, breathing Love.

When I first saw you as a baby — all ears and very long legs and those special toes, especially your "opposing thumb," I knew I had found my buddy. I became your human momma. Zephy, you helped me through my mother, Ida Marie's, death. You helped me feel again. I loved the day I found out you loved cantaloupe. I will pick the very best piece I can find and offer it up to you, so you will have all the things you love with you.

You were a kitty-puppy, always greeting me at the door or following me throughout the house. I must admit there were times I followed you, to let you know how much I adored you. I often said, "If only humans told each other how much they loved each other as much as I told you how handsome you are and how much I adored you, the world would be a much better place."

I loved how you would chat with me in so many tones. My big boy stretched out to three feet long and at his prime weighed eighteen lbs. You were a people-kitty. Never in a pushy way, but in your own gentle fashion. Sometimes I would come out on the porch and sit in the swing chair and up you would come while I read, and I'd tell you, "I love you so much, big boy." You would look up with those beautiful green eyes, shiny black coat and blue collar. I loved hearing you lope up the back porch steps, talking to me till you got to the top floor and saw me. Seeing you so peaceful, sleeping in the sun and the joy of seeing your sweet face whenever I opened the door gave me a sense of serenity. To have you sitting here now is my deepest wish.

Yesterday I went to the video store to get a film that a friend said might help, "What Dreams May Come," and doubled over in grief sobbing on the sidewalk. A woman stopped to see if I was okay, and I am not. Losing you Zephy is killing me. I am trying to do things to take care of my self... talking with friends, drinking water, eating when I can, still nauseous when I try to eat. I can't bear this pain and loss.

Zephy, you were my constant connection to love and beauty and sweetness for sixteen years. I miss your grace and guidance. I know people say this will pass, yet I feel crippled by this pain...for my soul and heart are struggling to bear this loss...the loss of my best friend in the world. At times I wish I could join you, but have been told I am not done here yet. It is a struggle, sweet boy. The pain I feel is proportionate to the love I have for you, thus immense. I adore and love you Zephy, my Handsome Boy... these are words you heard many times, every day of your life ... I pray you still hear them now.

Your Momma,
Leenie

Leenie Bachman
Massage Therapist
Jamaica Plain, Massachusetts

There is no need for a piece of sculpture
in a home that has a cat.

—Wesley Bates

Dogs

He is your friend, your partner, your defender, your dog.
You are his life, his love, his leader.
He will be yours, faithful and true,
to the last beat of his heart.
You owe it to him to be worthy
of such devotion.

—author unknown

ARROW

CHIHUAHUA MIX
8-MONTH-OLD MALE
MAY 11, 1998 - JANUARY 15,1999

To My Beloved Arrow,

You were born small and weak and people doubted that you would live, but this thought didn't cross my mind and basic instinct told me to be your foster parent. I accepted this challenge without thinking twice. I devoted 24 hours a day to you and endured sleepless nights in hopes of nurturing you to health. When you gained strength, everybody was amazed and the doubts faded. It's okay that you didn't grow to be very big, I loved every bit of your three-pound frame. What was important was that you were healthy. Your veterinarians said your growth would be stunted because of the lack of early nourishment. Nevertheless, I was more than overjoyed to call you my "Dwarfed Chihuahua."

Arrow, for eight months we enjoyed each other's company. Every hug, every cuddle and kiss was a pleasure, and I just couldn't get enough. Remember the car rides and the visits to Blockbuster Video? You made people smile. It was your size that they delighted in, not to mention your long ears and small button nose and eyes. You were so adorable. I can still see you eating your favorite foods: frosted mini-wheats and whipped cream. Oh, how you got messy with the whipped cream.

Sometimes I want to get angry at God for taking you on this cold, rainy morning. Instead, I want to apologize and ask for your forgiveness. Arrow, I am so sorry that our bedroom was in a loft where it was too steep for you. I am so sorry you fell and died instantly. I wish it was me to have fallen instead of you. The tremendous burden of guilt that I now carry is more than I can stand at times. It is hard not be depressed, sad and lonely. The pain and void in my heart are unbearable and sometimes I cry uncontrollably.

It's hard to understand why God chose to take you away from me after we had come so far, but I believe you came for a reason. Even through death you continue to touch our lives in miraculous ways. Before you were born, Daddy Mark and I forgot that there are important moral standards that we must live by in order to maintain a semblance of peace. Our marriage was in turmoil and we seemed to be angry all of the time. When you came into our lives, the negative barriers disappeared. Our hearts were melted as you showed us that devotion, commitment, loyalty and respect would be our saving grace. We are doing fine now and we owe it all to you.

In my sorrow and grief, I also feel that I am blessed. I am blessed with your memory which lives and reigns in my heart. In your honour, I will continue to believe that patience is a virtue, that friends are a pleasure, that families are a privilege and should be appreciated and that obstacles and hurdles can be conquered as long as you believe. Life is important and I don't take things for granted any longer. I am less neglectful, and I am mindful to keep criticism at a minimum.

I miss you, Arrow, more than words can describe, and though your existence on earth was short, I wouldn't have missed it for the world. I know I will be with you again to hold your sweet little head and kiss your cute button nose. Until we are together again, enjoy Rainbow Bridge and all of your friends and family. I hope there is plenty of frosted mini-wheats and whipped cream.

Your Mommy Forever,
Sandy

Sandy Hartunian
Secretary
Watsonville, California

BAMBI DORIS

MEXICAN COCKER SPANIEL
(We bought her in Mexico and they told
us she was a Cocker Spaniel, but...?)
9-YEAR-OLD FEMALE
OCTOBER, 1990 - JUNE 17, 1999

Dear Bambi!

Do you remember when we brought you home from the traveling bazaar in Mexico nine years ago? You were so young and scared you could barely stand up without wobbling, so we called you Bambi, like a newborn fawn. For the next five years you were the queen of our little town. There wasn't anyone who didn't know Bambi. The poultry man in the market saved chicken backs for the dog food concoctions the maid cooked every day (when she wasn't shooing you out of the kitchen with her broom). The butcher gave you thick meaty bones. And you proudly accompanied the kids after school each afternoon, through the sun-baked, dusty streets, to grandma's house for a friendly pat on the head, a siesta in the garden shade, a cool drink, and a treat.

Naughty Bambi, you escaped from the yard so many times for your romantic assignations with Coco. Do you remember following me around the house, whelping pups in the living room, until finally we settled down together and waited hours for the rest of your family to appear? Not long afterward, an economic crisis devastated the country and I lost my job. You may have been the first dog in Mexican history to support your human family: each of your puppies went to a fine home...and thus supplied enough money to buy groceries. One of them even sat beside the desk of the Consul General of the American Embassy in Italy!

Not much later, we were forced to return to our native Maryland. I could tell you thought you had landed in heaven. The smells! The squirrels! The deer! Long walks every day on fresh green lawns!

Splashing in the creek! And when you saw your first snowfall, you barked in alarm and confusion and excitement at the frosty intruders falling down from the sky.

Sadly, our family came apart in divorce, and we were forced to move from place to place. Once again, Bambi, you were instrumental in our rescue. When the nasty landlord's wife changed her mind about having pets in the house, she told us to get rid of you. But you introduced us to a kind neighbor (who loved dogs) who found us a smart real estate agent (who loved dogs) who made a miracle happen, and we BOUGHT you a house with a backyard in the forest, a nearby lake to chase geese into, and pesky squirrels to watch all day through the glass patio door. Home at last!

Becky likes to say you are our guardian angel. You fed us when we were hungry, found us a home when we had nowhere to go, and gave us comfort when our family unraveled. But maybe that's the reason you were sent to us ... to keep us going through dark times, and now that you have done your job, you are on your way to your own reward.

Thank you, Bambi Doris, for your adoring companionship, your mute understanding, and your unswerving conviction that each morning would bring a romp in the woods. You'll be with us always in our hearts and memories where we treasure the lifetime we shared.

The people who love you,
Susan, Becky, Jack, Anna
and Tiger, the tabby cat (who Becky says is YOUR guardian angel!)

Susan Zimmerman
Editor/Writer
Montgomery Village, Maryland

BENJI

CAVALIER KING CHARLES SPANIEL
8-YEAR-OLD MALE
MAY 24, 1989 - JULY 7, 1997

My Dear Benji,

You will never know how much I miss you and how you left your pawprints on my heart. I loved you so much. You were always a weak little dog somehow, always at the vet's, but you loved going to the vet's because he made you feel better and you knew that. We bought a king size bed for you and your three little companions, and you never went short of anything, especially love and affection.

The day you died I couldn't say goodbye because I wasn't there. I kissed you that morning and said, "See you at dinner time," but it wasn't to be. You quietly slipped away that day at 12:30, and all I saw of you, my baby, was a brown ear sticking out of a sheet when the pet ambulance came for you as I arrived home from work.

You had a bad little heart from the age of four, and you had to have medication every day. Your last holiday in Wales with us and your three little companions was sad because you couldn't join in and run about with them. You just lay in the shade and watched, because that summer was a very hot one. In fact, because you were not well and not yourself, we came home a day sooner than planned. I'll always remember driving home that day. You were on the back seat with your Dad, but you had your little head on my shoulder all the way home. I had to take my Auntie home on Sunday, and you wanted to come with us, but I thought it would be too hot for you in the car. I was going to take you to the vet's Monday afternoon, but it wasn't to be. You went under your own steam quietly and without a fuss. A dignified, enchanting little Cavalier right up to the end.

I hope, Benji, you are at the Rainbow Bridge now and waiting for me, because I promise you one day I will join you and hold your beautiful little body next to mine once more. Please God. Goodbye Benji, but not forever. I know you are waiting for me somewhere, just round the corner.

Love always, your Mum,
Dolores

Dolores M. Parker
Retired Civil Servant
Liverpool, England

I marvel that such small ribs as these
can cage such vast desire to please.

—Ogden Nash

— Photo by Agnes E. Canter

BENJI

POODLE/TERRIER MIX
11-YEAR-OLD MALE
OCTOBER 15, 1988 - SOON

Dear Benji,

I am feeling so helpless and sad that I can't do anything to help you. I may be wrong, and God only knows that, but doctors and my internal feelings are telling me that your life may not last long. I am angry. I cry so much, but nothing is helping. Not even medicines you are taking. The worse is that I feel like it's all my fault, that I didn't love you enough.

I never wanted to turn back the time, no matter how horrible I was feeling, but now I just wish that I can sit in a time machine and drive myself into November 29, 1988 when I first sneaked you into my house and showed you to Mom and Dad. You were so happy and cheerful that we decided to name you Benji (the son of happiness). And that's what you were to us all these years. Nothing but pure happiness. You managed to pull love out of everybody.

I will always remember the warmth of your body in the dark hours of the night when you would sneak into my bed and I would gladly let you under my blanket. I will always remember how you defended the small and weak ones. I will always remember your funny little tail that you used to greet us and make us feel loved. I will always remember your silent support when my Mom and Dad were having problems. And I will also remember your little jealousy when I would coddle another dog.

I forgive you for ruining my slippers, and I forgive you for stealing a ham from my sandwich. But what I can't forgive is the fact that you will abandon me soon. I can't forgive God for the fact that you are in great pain, and I will never, ever forgive myself for that day when I will have to put you to sleep. In my eyes I will be a murderer, even though maybe you will look at me as your deliverer.

I am so scared that I almost can't breathe. I feel like I could never, ever have another dog. You were so special that nobody can take your place. I just wish that you will forgive me for anything that you think I've done wrong, and I wish that you will always feel my endless love towards you.

I know you will be in paradise. You have a place there already waiting for you, which you deserve, being such a good dog. You stole my heart, and before you, I never knew I had one, so I thank you. Benji, my love for you is timeless.

Your friend,
Lana

Lana Bubenik
Sociology Student
Croatia, Europe

BENNY

DOBERMAN
(He weighed only 35 lbs. when rescued at age 12)
12-YEAR-OLD MALE
1986-SEPTEMBER 20, 1998

Benny,

I am so sorry for not being able to save you from your demons, but I hope I did help you forget, if even for just a moment, that you were ever without love. I also want to thank you for all you gave me.

When I think of that first day I met you, all I see is a skinny, trusting boy looking at me as if to say, "Do what you want to me, I'm here." I couldn't help the tears from falling on your sunburnt coat. And how proud I was of you on the long ride home! You were such a gentleman.

I think of how happy you seemed when you found not one, but two dogs waiting for you at your new house. Katie the Rott and little, sweet Sadie the other rescue Dobie. I know they were your first friends and how you loved to run with them in the yard. I thought my heart would break watching you learn to play. You found the joy of blankets and full dishes of food for the first time in your life. Watching you drag your blanket around was sure a sight.

I know that you thought we were your saviors, but in truth you were mine. You taught me the true meaning of "unconditional love." How you could still love and trust after the life you had amazes me. I took strength from you and learned what courage really is.

On our last day together I will always remember the calm strength you had as we walked into the vet's. As your doctor gave you the shot, you seemed happy to be going to a place with no bad memories. I know you are resting well and are finally at peace. I will always think of you with love. Even though our time together was short, you impacted many lives here, and your presence is still with us.

Rest well my friend, till we meet again at the Rainbow Bridge.
Sue
and Katie (Rottie)
and Sadie (rescue Dobie)

Sue Culberson
Phoenix, Arizona

—*Benny was a hospice dog I took in for Doberman Rescue here in Arizona. I had him for only six weeks, and he did more for me than I ever could have done for him. He had been abused for all of his twelve years. Understandably, he had many problems, both mental and physical, but he had a huge impact on my life. I would not take back even one day of our time together. Thanks to Benny I have decided to hospice more unadoptable Dobies or Rotties. He taught me that I can be strong enough to help other dogs by giving them a loving home for whatever time they have left and to be there for them when it's time for them to go on to a better place ... Sue*

BOWSER

ROTTWEILER/GERMAN SHEPHERD
5-MONTH-OLD MALE
FEBRUARY 16, 1999 - JULY 21, 1999

Oh Bowser,

I don't think you ever knew how much I love you. When I "rescued" you from our old neighbors, I thought I was giving you a great start for a new life. I didn't know that because I couldn't afford your vaccinations that it would cost you your life. I feel that it is somehow my fault that you got the parvo virus, although I know that I can't be blaming myself for this.

I never told you how much you meant to me. I took it for granted that you were always there to lie by me when I was sad, and when I was sick you slept beside me on the couch. You were the sweetest dog in the world, and I'm sorry that you didn't even get a chance to grow up.

I couldn't even be there when the vet gave you the shot. It would have given me nightmares for the rest of my life. But now I hate myself for leaving you with a stranger to die. I'm so sorry, honey. I know how scared you must have been. I hope you can forgive me for that.

I love you, Bowser, and I will never forget you. You helped me to survive one of the toughest times in my life. When I thought everyone was against me, you were there to lick my tears off of my face and to make me smile.

I'm sorry that we never got a chance to do all the things I wanted to do with you. I never got to take you to the beach on a nice day and let you play in the water. I never got to take you out to the country to let you run wild in the fields.

I want to ask for your forgiveness, Bowser. I never thought that your life would end so tragically and suddenly. On Monday you were playing with me in the backyard. By Wednesday you had passed away. I'll miss you forever, honey. You'll always be in my heart. I love you, Bowser.

Danica Kimberley
Student, age 16
Saskatoon, Saskatchewan, Canada

The one absolutely unselfish friend that man
can have in this selfish world,
the one that never deserts him,
the one that never proves ungrateful
nor treacherous, is his dog.

—George Graham Vest

BUTTONS

COLLIE/TERRIER MIX
17-YEAR-OLD MALE
DECEMBER 28, 1980 - APRIL 17, 1997

Dear Buttons,

It's been two years since you slipped away quietly in your sleep, and still your presence in our lives and in our family is so strong, and it always will be. You left a legacy that stands the test of time. You were loving confidante, protector, baby-sitter, playmate, comforter, hero, and above all else, you were the truest of friends.

It was so hard to say goodbye, and I think you understood that, and felt it in your own way also. I sensed your struggle those last few days, your body so tired and weak, but you were fighting to live for us. You were trying to be strong until you knew we'd be okay. In your eyes, you were growing weary of the battle.

One night I lay awake, worrying about you, sensing that you were waiting for something and yet not sure I had to courage to grant it to you yet. But I didn't want you to suffer. I didn't trust myself to make the decision, and turned it over again and again in my mind, whether or not we needed to take you to the vet the next day or not. I prayed silently and with many tears that God take you, if that was what you needed, and that He take you without fear and pain, and with all the dignity that we wanted for you. I knew we would never be fully ready, but I understood that you were so loyal that you would give us your all, and then some, until we let you go. You were such a good dog. You loved so completely, and I think we came to realize that it was because we loved you to that extent in return, that it was time to let you go, and that you needed permission...your loyalty and spirit still as strong as the day we were blessed with you, a small bundle of mischief and fire, joining our lives.

That night we remembered all the things that were uniquely you. Morning rituals of you grabbing a sock or a glove as we struggled to get ready for school, ending in mad chases around and around the table until Mom was ready to scream. The time you pulled down an entire clothesline of wash, and years later, the stash of socks we found buried under the big bush in the yard. The love you had for running through the grass with a hula-hoop, bigger than you, trying to goad someone into a game of tug-o-war. (We still have that hula hoop, complete with your signature teeth marks in it.) The way you crossed your paws to look elegant, and the language you spoke that at times seemed almost human ... all the ways you touched our lives for which we will always be grateful, and which can never be forgotten, which will hold a tight grip on our hearts forever.

The next morning, I woke just as your breathing slowed to a stop, and your dreams carried you into a new place, where things weren't a struggle anymore and you could do all that you did when you were just that tiny ball of fur. We miss you more than words can express, Buttons, but you knew it was time, and we needed to honor that and honor you. We continue to do that, as you are alive in our hearts and in our memories, always, and your presence never fades. At times I see you in my dreams, and I know you will be waiting one day for us, in a wonderful place where we will someday be all together again. You are dearly loved, and dearly missed, and lovingly remembered.

With love always,
Debra, Lynn, Susan, Mommy and Daddy

Debra Rotanz
College Student
Shallotte, North Carolina

CC DOLL

COCKER SPANIEL
11-YEAR-OLD FEMALE
JANUARY 19, 1988 - MAY 26, 1999

A Love Letter to my Darling Dog, CC Doll,

Today is 30 days since you left me in tears and a broken heart. I look at your beautiful pictures and you look back with your wonderful love. The miss and hurt is almost more than I can stand — I cry all the time. You meant so much in my life and in our life together.

Each time I look out the window where you are, I throw you many tearful kisses and put a fresh flower on you every day. I miss cleaning your eyes every morning and getting your kisses for doing it for you, my sweetheart.

Molli Girl and Star Baby (my cats) always leave a bit of food for you to lick up. Molli Girl also leaves a little milk for you in her bowl. When I go outside to throw out paper or garbage, Molli Girl comes looking for you; she misses you and our walks.

You received lots of loving cards and flowers from all your friends: your groomer, your vets, the cat taxi and the people in the apartment. Jim upstairs said a prayer for you and we had a lovely eulogy read. CC Doll, I gave away your food stuff, but all your toys, pillow, cage, collar and chain are all in your place. I don't want to change anything.

I try to remember all the good times we had together, and I would not have wanted to miss that for the world. We had a wonderful life together — eleven years and four months. The loss is deep, but the memories are strong and beautiful, my love, CC Doll.

Love, Hugs & Kisses Forever,
Your Mother

Agnes E. Canter
Portland, Oregon

CHAMP

LABRADOR/SHEPHERD MIX
14½-YEAR-OLD MALE
FEBRUARY 19, 1983 - SEPTEMBER 13, 1997

It is one year ago today that you made your journey to the Rainbow Bridge. The pain of losing you has eased over the year and is replaced by all the wonderful memories I have of you. I remember bringing you home — you were just a little ball of fur and so adorable.

You grew so rapidly that you developed hip dysplasia. The vet didn't give you much hope of living past seven years old, but you sure proved him wrong. The vet was amazed how well you were doing. You were still taking two-mile walks at thirteen years. At two years you developed a lump on your side that turned out to be cancerous. Once again you were a fighter — went through chemo and did really well. You then developed skin allergies and I had to learn to give you monthly shots. How you loved your shots — you always got a special treat for being so good.

You were just like a child when it came to Christmas. You had your own wrapped gifts and knew which were yours. You wouldn't touch them till they were given to you and then you would tear off the paper into a million pieces and play with your new toys to your heart's content. You used to love to eat corn-on-the-cob just like a person. There were two spots on the kitchen floor that for some reason you felt the need to walk backwards — you just couldn't walk normal on those two spots — you always had us laughing. You loved when we had visitors — you would grab a toy and bring it to them to play with you. You would not be ignored. When it was time for our visitors to leave, you would run to the door and bark as if to say, "Please don't leave yet."

The last two months of your life were not kind to you. Your hips began to give out more and more. You started to lose control of your bladder and Mommy had to hand feed you. I struggled with trying to decide when to say "good-bye," but you would always bring me a toy and want to play.

Finally, the last night you couldn't get your hind legs up. I looked into your eyes and could see you were no longer happy — so I gave you a big hug and told you I loved you and that I would be brave and let you go with the intention of calling the vet in the morning to put you to sleep. You took that decision away from me and went to the Bridge during the night. My deepest regret is that I was not there to hold you while you made your journey — for that I am deeply sorry!

My Friend, Companion and Protector — I miss you and will always love you!

Till we meet again,
Mommy

Ruth Drake
Clerk / Typist
Seaside Heights, New Jersey

Our companion animals offer us security, succor, esteem,
understanding, forgiveness, fun and laughter, and most
importantly, abundant and unconditional love.

—Leo Bustad

CHANCE

YELLOW LAB MIX
10-MONTH-OLD MALE
UNKNOWN - JANUARY 23, 1999

Chance,

My sweet boy, I miss you more than I thought possible. You were supposed to be with me for years to come; your death was so untimely. I pray that you didn't suffer, Chancey.

Did you hear me calling you? We did everything in our power to find you. A neighbor found your body, baby. She knew for sure that it was you because you were still wearing your orange collar that you got from Santa for Christmas. Do you remember that last night that we were together? I need you to always remember the last words I said to you before I went inside that night. I told you how much I loved you and that I would see you in the morning. Then I gave you your good-night kiss on top of your head. Never has a dog captured my heart as quickly and completely as you did!

I know, without a doubt, that you are waiting for me at Rainbow Bridge. I will be reunited with you, Bud. I don't know when, but I will be there; I promise. I know that you have Harry, Brandy, and now Gator too, to keep you company.

Thank you, Chance, for allowing me the time I needed with Gator here on Earth before sending for him. You know that both he and his sister, Rosie, came here six months ago in search of you, their playmate, their friend. I promised you then, right after you went to the Bridge, that I would do all that I could for them because they were your friends.

I will miss Gator terribly, but in a way I am happy for him. He achieved his goal. Don't forget how much I love you, my butterball, and have lots of fun. Rest In Peace, Chance, until we meet again... and please give this message to Gator for me:

My good friend, Gator, what began as a promise I made to Chance quickly turned into a privilege. Chance will now take over for me; watching over you, where I was forced to leave off. Thank you, Gator, from the bottom of my heart, for allowing me to become part of your time here on Earth. I know it took much courage on your part to become as close to me as you did. Rather than call you my "pet," I would say that you were my very good friend. I am honored to have accompanied you on your quest.

When you and Rosie came to me in search of Chance it was, no doubt, the lowest point in my life, and yours also. We needed each other. You needed good food, a comfortable place to sleep, and above all some human contact. I needed something to distract me from the grief and guilt I felt over Chance's death. I taught you how to play, how to trust, and most importantly, that not all humans are cruel. You taught me how to laugh again.

You can Rest in Peace now, Gator. You came into my world in search of your friend, Chance, and you have finally found him. You are finally playing with him once again; what you really only wanted in the first place. I just kind of got in the middle of your journey. I promise to take good care of Rosie. She has become very special to me. In her, I still have a little bit of you. I don't want to say good-bye. It sounds too final. Think of this as a temporary arrangement. Our time together has not ended; it has only just begun.

Both of you have taught me that the best things in life are not saved for or even planned...they just happen, and that some friendships never end. I will never fear leaving this life, because some of the kindest souls I have ever met already have, and they are patiently awaiting my arrival. See you boys at the Bridge...

Judy Miller
Homemaker
Ray City, Georgia

CHANCE

SHEPHERD/LABRADOR
14-YEAR-OLD MALE
OCTOBER 1981 - OCTOBER 9, 1995

Dear Chance,

It seems strange to write you a letter, and even though I've written and re-written it so many times in my mind, I'm still unsure about how the words will actually come out. This sure isn't easy. But I know that the past couple of months haven't been easy for you, either.

You have so much heart and will to survive, but I've watched it slip away. They say I'm supposed to know when you're ready to go. For a long time I just didn't believe that. I thought that even if you said the words out loud, I wouldn't hear them. I wouldn't allow myself to. But I'm realizing that sometimes the kindest help one can give is the permission for a loved one to go. I asked you to please let me know when that time is, Chance, because I was afraid I wouldn't be able to see it without your help. I'm listening, and although it's difficult to accept, I hear what you're telling me now.

I keep remembering when you showed up at my door with such wide, young, trusting eyes. You've been such a constant and dependable part of my life for fourteen years. You've been beside me and loved me even at my low points. Even when it was sometimes difficult to love myself. You showed me what unconditional love, friendship and companionship are, and I'll always love you for sharing that with me and for choosing me to be your lifetime friend.

The other evening I watched you while you slept. You must have been dreaming because your legs were moving. I remembered when I used to joke that you were chasing rabbits. I watched your feet twitch and listened to your whimpers and cried because I knew that you'd never run again. I wanted you to go on dreaming forever.

I want so much to do what's right for you and whatever will keep your last days here peaceful. I'm trying so hard not to be selfish and hold on to you longer than you want to be held. I want what you want, Chance, and if that means closing your eyes and leaving this world, then it's okay. I'll know you won't be hurting anymore. I'll know that you'll be running in the pasture, dozing in the sunshine, chasing rabbits and being our kitties' best friend. I'll know that the sparkle will be back in your eyes, and that you'll be happy. I'll know that you will again, and forever, be the Chance I had the privilege of knowing for fourteen years. Please know that I'll always feel your presence with me, and I'll always be right beside you, too.

We'll be together again, I know. So I'll say goodbye only for now. Thank you, Chance. For everything.

I love you,
Laura

COCO

SHELTIE MIX
9-YEAR-OLD FEMALE
UNKNOWN - JANUARY 13, 1997

To My Precious CoCo:

I remember the day you were brought to me. It was the Sunday after Thanksgiving, and little did I know what a wonderful Thanksgiving gift you would come to be. Someone had left you and your puppies when they moved, and you were brought to me ... a scared little brown dog with no hair on your tail and a very serious problem with your eye. You were one-half or more Sheltie. You had one ear up and one ear down.

I took you to see Dr. Maret. He confirmed what I had thought...you had to have your eye removed. You also needed to be spayed and have your rear dew claws removed. I was so worried that I called the office at least ten times. You had sutures everywhere, but you didn't cry once. I put a blanket and pillow beside the couch. I also put your water and food there so you wouldn't have to go too far. I slept on the couch to make sure you didn't need anything. You licked my hand when you needed to go out.

After I had given you a good flea bath, that skinny little tail became a beautiful plume. You had become very settled in. All you had to put up with was Samantha the cat. She would chase you and then you would chase her. You made more noise in your sleep than you did when you were awake. The first year that we were together, you really worked yourself into my heart. You were my baby.

In February of 1994, five weeks and one day after Mom had passed away, we lost your Daddy. When I helped him get dressed to go to the hospital, his bathrobe was just thrown on the end of the bed. When he died, Aunt Jean and Uncle John were going to take me to their house, but I said we had to come home to feed you and Shawney, Mom's Collie. When we came in, you went to the door and looked for Daddy. You came and jumped in my lap, and I just buried my face in your fur and told you Daddy wasn't coming home anymore. I saw a tear in that one eye of yours. You licked the tears from my face. You slept on Daddy's bathrobe that night. You were still Daddy's Little Princess. Because of you, Shawney and Samantha, I did not come home to an empty house.

In March of 1996, you started having trouble. I had to take you to have ultrasounds of your heart and kidneys. The report was not good. You had your good and bad days. You would get in my lap, and I could feel your heart miss a beat. You did pretty well until December of 1996 when your heart and kidneys worsened. You had to spend two weekends at Dr. Maret's. Down deep I knew we wouldn't be together much longer. The last weekend that you were with me, you had stopped eating. I laid on the floor and held you. On Monday morning I called Dr. Maret's office. You had told me with that little brown eye that it was time, but I needed to hear from Dr. Maret that there was nothing else I could do. He confirmed what I knew, and I couldn't see you suffer any longer. We had been through too much together. I was holding you and telling you how much I loved you, and again that brown fur was holding my tears. I also asked you to tell your Daddy and my Mom how much I loved them and how I missed them. You went to the Bridge with my arms around you.

You are in a safe place now. I know someday you will see me at the Bridge and come running to me, and things will be as they were before. I will always love and miss Daddy's Little Princess.

Cindy

Cindy Readle
Indianapolis, Indiana

A dog has the soul of a philosopher.

—Plato

CRUISER

MIXED BREED DOG
12-YEAR-OLD FEMALE
FEBRUARY 1986 - NOVEMBER 1998

Dear Cruiser,

We all miss you here in Antigonish. You are remembered with love by many people in town, and everybody I meet has a funny tale to tell me about you.

Craig drew a beautiful picture of you and gave it to me for Christmas this year. When we saw it, we all cried, but now it has become one of my most prized belongings, second only to my memories of you.

My only regret about your life is that you could not be there to meet and greet all of my new friends. They will never understand what a wonderful life you were.

Did you know that the only time I ever saw Dad cry was at your burial? You meant a lot to all of us. I believe you chose your own time to pass, and I believe you told me, somehow, to prepare. I puzzle over the way you died; crossing the street as in any other day, following my sister in trust that she would protect you. It is ironic that the very trust we gave you in people is the reason for your death.

I will never forget you, Cruiser, and I never want to. Someday we will meet again in heaven, and you can play and console and comfort like you were gifted to do.

Love always,
Rosalyn

Rosalyn MacDonald
Student of Veterinary Medicine
Charlottetown, Prince Edward Island, Canada

CUBBIE

MALTESE
7-YEAR-OLD MALE
JANUARY 14, 1992 - APRIL 14, 1999

Cubbie,

Can you hear me? Can you see me? Do you know how I long to feel you in my arms?

You were always there for me. Always at my side. Those big brown eyes, your soft snowy fur. All a comfort to me. What you gave me can never, ever be replaced. You were my reason for waking each day. My companion, at night. Going to sleep is not the same. I call to you ... expecting, hoping to see your little spirit run to me. To see your tail wagging ... and the joy in your eyes ... just because you love me. How can I face each day without you??

It is too quiet. My heart aches ... my soul cries ... to feel you in my arms. To know that you are ok ... safe ... that was my job. And I can't be there. If I could ... please know ... oh, I would.

You will never be forgotten ... as you are etched upon my soul. Thank you for your love, companionship, and incredible joy. You are part of me...I am never too far away ... call to me ... and know my soul will always answer. I love you, Cubbie ... and would give the world to just hold you again ... to look into your eyes ... to smell your skin ... God Bless you ... and keep you safe ... My sweet missed baby ...

I adore you ...
Mommy

Joanne Mooney-King
IBM
Tampa, Florida

DARTH "POOHBEAR"

ENGLISH COCKER SPANIEL
5-YEAR-OLD MALE
JUNE 1993 - OCTOBER 21, 1998

Dear PoohBear,

For five years you brightened our lives and loved us without question, and now you have left us. I miss you, dear heart, and everyone else that knew you is so very sad that you are no longer here.

Patton looked for you for a very long time ... I still look for you almost every day when I get home.

You were the best boy anyone could ever ask for, so bright and sweet ... the world is a little darker without you.

Until the day we meet again, my best boy, I will hold you in my heart. ...

Should you go first and I remain, one thing I'd have you do:
walk slowly down that long, lone path, for soon I'll follow you.
I'll want to know each step you take that I may walk the same,
for some day down that lonely road
you'll hear me call your name.

—A.K. Rowswell

Love,
Mommy

Michaela Payne
Maxwell, Iowa

Dogs are not our whole lives,
but they make our lives whole.

—Roger Caras

DOLLY

TOY POODLE
11-YEAR-OLD FEMALE
APRIL 16, 1987 - DECEMBER 26, 1998

Dolly,

You were a great little girl. You were a natural born retriever. You fetched our daily paper and anything else you could carry. Though only fifteen pounds, you could climb the steps with the heavy, bulky Sunday paper. You could pull in our stringer loaded with fish...even if we were not quite ready for that!

You knew your toys by name and would bring them on request. I can still see your soft little body stretched out on the hearth in frog-fashion. I can see you in the garden moseying down the rows of veggies looking for a bell pepper or a choice green bean. You always picked them so very carefully. I see your little gray body blending in with the weathered gray boards of the fence as you patrolled the backyard.

Dolly, I still step over your bed beside mine. I hear your soft breathing as you slept by my side...oh, how I miss you. You recognized many, many words and commands. We never once needed to scold you. You seemed almost naturally house-trained when we brought you home at about two months of age.

You hiked mountain trails, went to the bank with us for treats, went everywhere we went, and though never roaming far, always coming at our call. You loved to be outside, BUT only if we were. You intertwined yourself around our hearts...and loved "Dad" and me equally. We are so lost without you...but we are striving to remember the wonderful twelve years we had together.

You were so very pretty, silver and white, not desired in competition, but a champion in beauty, intelligence, charm and love. You will always be in our hearts, Dolly... and never forgotten.

"Mom" and "Dad"

Doe Edwards
Homemaker / Secretary
Liberal, Kansas

DOT

BORDER COLLIE
5-YEAR-OLD FEMALE
NOVEMBER 21, 1990 - JANUARY 15, 1995

Dot,

You were taken from me and I did not know why. My heart and spirit broke. But now I know by the Grace of God, it was not to be; you had to be taken from me for me to live. Thank you talking to God, for sending me Slip and Abby. It was time. Bless you Dot, and I will see you one day, when it is time again.

Love,
Ann

Ann Humbertson
Dog Trainer
Oldtown, Maryland

DUFFY

SHEPHERD MIX
13-YEAR-OLD MALE
JUNE 7, 1986 - JULY 10, 1999

My Dear Duffy,

I remember the day Mike brought you home from the Dayton Humane Society. How frightened you were. You had been badly abused, had mange and badly in need of a good meal. Our other dog, Jenny, adopted you, and it was love at first sight for both of you. The next day we took you to the vet. That was thirteen years ago. You never got over being fearful of people. The only ones that could pet you were the family. You would hide under the table whenever we had company.

What a sweet, loving, funny guy you were. You gave us so much pleasure. We loved you every day. You passed away two nights ago, and we miss you so much. If there is a doggie heaven, I know you will meet Jenny there.

We love you always,
Mom and Dad

Ellie Kaufman
Columbus, Ohio

Animals are such agreeable friends.
They ask no questions, they pass no criticisms.

—George Eliot

EBONY

COCKER SPANIEL
12-YEAR-OLD FEMALE
JUNE 1987 - APRIL 28, 1999

Ebony,

I miss you so much. You were my best friend and I couldn't have asked for a better dog. I will always have a place for you in my heart. We will play again one day.

I love and miss you,
Paula

Paula Burge
Health Care Provider
Mansfield, Ohio

FROSTY MORNING

LONGCOAT CHIHUAHUA
10-YEAR-OLD FEMALE
MARCH 25, 1973 - NOVEMBER 26, 1982

Dear Frosty...

How can I write a letter to you, who were heart of my heart and soul of my soul? My sweet, perfect little girl. It's been over sixteen years since you went away to Rainbow Bridge, and yet it was only yesterday. I've never tried to write to you before. There's so much to tell you, I don't know where to start. I know you know how much I loved you — how much I still love you. Do you remember the first time we saw each other?

Remember your daddy? At first he didn't think he wanted a dog. But you knew better, didn't you? You knew he wouldn't be able to resist you ... and of course he couldn't. Nobody could. By the end of the second day, he was calling you "Frosty Baby," and you were in.

You were the most incredibly intelligent dog I'd ever encountered. You never really needed to be trained because you always just knew what to do. I don't think I ever had to correct you more than once about anything...except knocking over wastebaskets. I guess every dog has to have one weakness, and wastebaskets were yours. I know you understood every word that was ever said to you ... you proved that again and again...and yet you listened to all my secrets, you kissed me when my heart was broken, you loved me when I felt like no one else did. You were all the unconditional, beautiful love in the world.

You were also the sweetest-natured dog I ever saw...you loved everyone. Well, nearly everyone. You didn't much care for salesmen or repairmen, because they didn't belong in your domain. And you always knew the difference between them and people who were friends. You guarded your home zealously... but you made friends with our friends and begged shamelessly for all the attention you could get.

That beautiful sweet spirit of yours carried over into all your off-spring, too. I could look into the eyes of every Frosty puppy that followed and see you there.

Your years here were too few... and a piece of me died the day you left me. I know it was your time... but it seemed very fitting that it was a dark, rainy day. That was when I found out that the angels could cry for a little dog... their tears fell in the rain that day. And mine still fall for you too, even though I know you have a beautiful home now at Rainbow Bridge, and I know I see your eyes shining in the stars at night. I know your love is still there, still real... and I know that we'll be together again someday. In the meantime, I still see you in my memories, as clearly as though it were only yesterday... and I love you, baby.

Forever ... Mom

Dee Gurnett
Secretary
San Antonio, Texas

GEMMA

GOLDEN RETRIEVER
9-YEAR-OLD FEMALE
OCTOBER 28,1989 - MARCH 24,1999

Dear Gemma,

You were my first dog, and you were the best thing in my life. You were my friend, and I miss you terribly. I still hear you and smell you and feel you, and I cannot bear to think of the empty years ahead without your company.

You were so much a part of our family. You knew our moods and movements before we did, and then at Christmas you suddenly developed lumps. "They are only fatty tissue lumps," everyone said. "All old dogs get them." So we ignored them. Then when there were so many, we took you to the vet. After they had done a biopsy, they said it was cancer of the lymph system and that it was very bad; you would not live until Easter. They were right.

I am so sorry, my dear friend, that I didn't take you to the vet sooner. We may have been able to do something. I will never forgive myself for that. But your last weeks were good. We stored up a lot of memories, and I know you knew how much we loved you. Thank you for nine wonderful years. I shall never forget you.

Sue

Sue Carsey
Burniston, Scarborough, England

GOLDA

ENGLISH BULLDOG
13½-YEAR-OLD FEMALE
FEBRUARY 14, 1982 - NOVEMBER 10,1995

Dear Golda,

I need to write to you and tell you that I think of you daily and will always remember the years we spent together and how joyous you made my life for so many years.

I remember the day you came to me and your new home. It was over Memorial Day weekend, and Dad and I surprised your two human sisters with you, and they were thrilled! You were so cute...all of about twenty lbs, and a cast on your left hind leg from falling off a moving vehicle. That person brought you to Phil and Lloyd, and when they became your legal guardians they called me. Now you are mine!!!!!!

I brought you home where you were introduced to your Boston Terrier brother, Bubba. You instantly knew that he was in charge, and you were a very gracious lady to him and loved him very much. Did you know that you were instrumental in his living for such a long time? Thank you.

I became aware that you and I shared a very special bond. We could communicate without words, mostly with just a look or a touch. I knew when you were not well, I knew all your moods and all of your likes and dislikes. Dad never could figure that out and would often laugh at us, calling us "spooky." But he became a believer when I had to have surgery. You stayed by my side, and then after the surgery, you stayed on the bed with me, careful not to bump into the side where the benign tumor had been removed. You left me for only potty-outings and food.

Did I ever tell you how much I loved to cuddle you? You always made me feel safe and warm...understanding all my problems and worries. You were the best listener! Then in November of 1995, you became quite ill. You would not eat and never moved from the couch.

Your pink tummy was gray, and your paws were cold to the touch. I brought you to Phil and Lloyd, and the girls came because we all knew that it didn't look good. Uncle Phil and Uncle Lloyd ran all the tests that they could. You were wonderful.

After all the tests were in, I knew what was about to happen, and you told me, "It's okay, Mom, I love you." Do you remember the puppy stories I told you about yourself and about all the things we did together? I held you and loved you and kissed you until you fell asleep, and then I stayed to make sure that you were comfortable. That was one of the saddest days of my life. I went home without you and cried for days. I slept with your picture and still talked to you, asking your advice on things. When I came home that day, your Pug brother, Cajunn, was distraught. He was missing you and would lay for hours on your couch.

I know that you are in a much better place, playing with your brother, Bubba, and now playing with Grandma Reggie. You made my life so wonderful and so rewarding. Thank you for always being there for me and for the family. I miss you so much and wish that I could love you and hold you and pet you one last time, but I know that is impossible.

Take care, my wonderful girl. Run and bark and play and eat all your favorite foods. You so loved bananas. I will see you in my dreams, and know that there is no other dog that can, or will, ever replace you....

I love you and miss you with all my heart,
Mom

Ellen H. Levy
Sign Language Interpreter / Teacher
Long Beach, California

Animals share with us the privilege of having a soul.

—Pythagoras

GUS

SPRINGER SPANIEL
9-YEAR-OLD MALE
UNKNOWN - JUNE 7, 1993

Hi Gus,

As you and I both know, you were never my pet, but instead, my Guardian Angel. As far as the ownership issue goes, it was you who owned me. At any rate, I have decided to write to you because I wish to pay tribute to such a great friend.

We met in 1989 when you came to live with a farmer I did accounting for. That Thanksgiving I volunteered to take care of you while your owner and his wife spent the holidays with family. You and I drove from Seattle to Pullman to visit a friend of mine who was going to school there. We left on the Wednesday before Thanksgiving and by Friday I knew you were going to be mine. When I returned to work the following Tuesday at the farm I didn't take you with me. I told the farmer I could not part with you because we had bonded and he agreed to let me have you. (I used some tears to persuade him but so what.) I had no idea at that time what a great impact you would have on my life.

We spent our time walking near the water in many different parks that bordered on the Puget Sound, playing ball, your favorite pastime, and going for rides in the car. You went everywhere with me. You slept on the bed with your head on the pillow next to my pillow, you listened to my complaints, comforted me when I was unhappy, and you never failed to be overjoyed when you saw me. When friends and family invited me to come over they always said, "Be sure to bring Gus." You were such a cut up sometimes that you eventually got the nickname "Goose." We even had our professional portrait done together at the suggestion of a friend. It is truly one of my most beloved treasures now.

You got very sick with pancreatitis in November 1991 and we

spent a great deal of time with many different vets and specialists. You would rally and then get deathly ill again. I was so terrified of losing you, and you sensed it. You would come and lay right near me and look at me with those big brown eyes and show me the love that came from your soul. The doctors finally figured out that the pred-nisone we had you on was causing the pancreatitis and when we discontinued it, you got better. Life returned to normal.

We moved to Oregon in February 1993 and stayed with a friend for a short period of time until we could find a place of our own. I bought a house in April, but it would be three months before we could move in. But you, my dearest friend, never made it. I believe to this day that you stayed long enough to know that I would be okay and then you left.

In early May, I took you to the emergency vet because you were not eating and you weren't your frisky self. He felt a huge mass in your stomach and said it should be x-rayed. On Monday I went to work and took you with me. On my break I took you to our regular vet who was two blocks from my office. He said there wasn't much point in doing an x-ray because he could feel the mass and the only way to identify it was to operate. He called me when the surgery was completed and I got to the office in about five minutes with my heart in my throat. The news was not good. It was cancer. I asked him how long you had, but what I really meant was, how long did I have before you would be gone from me. A totally selfish response, and when he said two to six months I was devastated. I took you home and vowed to make the most of the next six months.

When you were cold, I would cover you with my old Indian blan-ket and you would sleep curled up to my back. About two weeks later, you became listless and lost your appetite again. After some blood tests, the vet said you weren't doing as well as he had ex-pected and he feared that your time would be much shorter than the two to six months he had first predicted. He assured me that you would let me know when it was time to go.

What would I do without you as my constant companion? How

would I get by, and how could I come home each night without you here to greet me? We spent that last weekend with you sleeping and me trying to keep my mind on my book. It was a futile attempt at keeping reality at bay. I laid my head on your tummy and wept, not for you but for me. When I lifted my head up, you licked my tears. You were always my comfort and proof to me that animals have souls.

Monday morning June 7th, 1993, there was no more denial for me. I knew what I had to do and made the call to the vet. We would meet at 3 p.m. You laid your head on my shoulder and pressed very hard against me with your chest and gave me your last kiss. It was all very quick and you died in my arms, peacefully, quietly, and gracefully, just as you had lived. I buried my face in the soft fur of your side and wept without a sound for what seemed like an eternity. My heart felt as if it would explode, and the finality of your lifeless form in my arms was so overwhelming. You touched so many lives in the three-and-a-half years we spent together, Gussie, most of all mine, and I'm thankful to God for that.

The vet said you deserved to be buried some place special and since I did not have one, he took you to his farm and buried you under a beautiful oak tree on his property. That's where he buried you. I buried you in my heart. And here you stay.

Annie Robert
Accountant
McMinnville, Oregon

HANNAH

ROTTWEILER
9½-YEAR-OLD FEMALE
JUNE 1989 - APRIL 15, 1999

Hannah,

Today I let you go to a better place ... a place where you will no longer suffer from any kind of illness. I am sad and still crying, but I know I did the right thing. We did so many different things together since you were a tiny, fluffy, growling pup. Some things I made you do, like all those dumb tricks and all the searching I made you do when I hid from you. You never were angry at me for any of them. You only licked me and did what I asked. I am sorry you jumped into the stream thinking I was in trouble. I know you did not like the water, but you did it anyway. Thank you, girl.

I will never forget the times you sat by me when I was sad and the times I was mad at everyone or anything or even you. You still gave me unconditional love, and the only thing you wanted from me was a pat on the head or to curl up next to me. I miss you!!!

I'm still very sorry I could not be with you until the end. I wanted to be there when the vet gave you your...I feel like I abandoned you when you needed me the most. I am glad, though, that you got to have one last ride in my car because I know it is what you liked best. You got to sit in the front where you like to be.

It may seem like I am rambling on, girl, but it is hard to cry and type at the same time. I know you understand. I love you and already miss you and will always remember you. I am sorry.

Love,
Ann

Ann Stroman
Indian Springs, Nevada

HOK HOONG

CHOW/ESKIMO
5-YEAR-OLD FEMALE
UNKNOWN - FEBRUARY 18,1999

Dear Hok Hoong,

I gave you a Chinese name meaning "black bear" because you looked like one. We adopted you from the Humane Society on May 1, 1995. I knew my deceased dad had something to do with this because you were put on hold, but the people decided they didn't want you. So we adopted you. You were a stray; they guessed you were one-and-a-half to two years old.

I miss you soooo much. The house is so empty without you. Thank you for the unconditional love you gave us, especially me. You were a gift from God & Pop. They knew I was lonely after Dad's death. You helped me with my depression, particularly that first cold & snowy winter we had you. You made me go outside to get much needed exercise, sunshine & fresh air. You taught me to be responsible for someone other than myself. I fed, walked, trained, drove and played with you. You gave more than you were given.

I miss your smile, happy face, silky soft fur, wagging tail, puppy whine, low "woof" of a bark and silly antics (such as chasing your tail around and around) that made me laugh each day. I wish I could kiss the crease in your forehead and smell your ears again. I think of you every day and look at your favorite places (next to the large bush in the backyard, under our bedroom window, next to the sliding glass door in the family room and the corner behind your Dad's recliner). I remember how you trotted with your tail happily and proudly carried over your back.

I was so proud of you when we attended obedience school. I was ecstatic when we earned your Mixed Breed Novice, a Companion Dog title. It was one of the happiest moments of my life.

Chicken was your favorite food. You loved when I made home-made chicken soup & gave you the scraps. I remember what fun and laughs we had when you put your head in ice cream containers to lick them out. After earning the CD title, I took you out for your own dish of frozen vanilla custard, which I had promised.

I'm glad I kept a journal of your life with us. I still write in it about you. So many memories in so short a time. We didn't have you for four years, but you'll remain forever in our hearts. Originally you were MY dog, but you won over your Dad. You were such a good, loving dog that he wanted another one — a tribute to having the best first.

We adopted another Chow mix in April. Spock is not a replace-ment since no one could ever replace you. You were our first dog — MY very first one. You will always hold the honor of being my first doggy "daughter." I love you very, very much.

I'm grateful for the last gifts you gave me — allowing me to say "good-bye" and dying naturally. You have given me the lasting gifts of love, happy memories, knowing I can take care of and love a pet, acceptance and belief that I will see you again at the Rainbow Bridge. Until then, know that I love you and miss you.

Love Always,
Your Mom,
Nora

Nora Taranowski
Homemaker
Greendale, Wisconsin

HOLLY

YORKSHIRE TERRIER
14-YEAR-OLD FEMALE
UNKNOWN - DECEMBER 1998

Dear Holly,

When we (Master and I) took you from the shelter, an abused, frightened seven-year-old with no hair growing on your back, we felt pity and concern. We saw you at the shelter one day, thought about it and went back the next day to adopt you.

You were a nippy little thing because you had learned not to trust anyone. I was bitten a couple of times before you got used to me. With time you learned to trust and would come jumping into my lap and lick my fingers.

Seven years after you came to live with me, you got very sick and nothing we could do seemed to help. I finally helped you to the Bridge comforted with the thought that Master was waiting there to greet you. I miss you both but at least you have each other's company.

Mom

Barbara Madison
Retired
Cherry Hill, New Jersey

In order to really enjoy a dog,
one doesn't merely try to train him to be semi-human.
The point of it is to open oneself to the possibility
of becoming partly a dog.

—Edward Hoagland

IGOR

LHASA APSO
16-YEAR-OLD MALE
NOVEMBER 9, 1979 - MAY 24, 1995

Dear Iggy-Piggy,

I doubt if you'll ever see this, because I'm skeptical about the existence of life after death. It doesn't matter, though, because if there's even one chance in a zillion you might, then it's worth writing. (I suspect you can't read English, anyway. But I don't know Tibetan, so we're at an impasse, right?)

I miss you terribly, you know that, don't you. Having you near me was a blessing that I can never replace. No, I haven't gotten another pet now that you're gone. No one could ever take your place.

You gave us bushels of love and happiness. You also gave us plenty of tsuris and agita, of course, usually because you insisted on doing things your way regardless of what we thought. That's OK. That's part of what made you so extraordinarily special. And that's also part of the reason you will never ever be forgotten.

You will live in our minds and our hearts forever. I'm writing this, but we both know that Elisabeth will always love you at least as much as I do.

Your pal and buddy forever,
Larry

Larry Ritter
Teacher / Writer
New York, New York

JAMES

STANDARD POODLE
8½-YEAR-OLD MALE
NOVEMBER 5, 1990 - JUNE 19, 1999

Dear James,

Saturday, June 19, 1999

How can I describe the terrible loss I feel today when I left the veterinarian with your collar and leash in my hand? The empty feelings began from the moment I realized that you will never sit next to me, that I will never feel your beautiful cream-colored coat, or look into your intelligent brown eyes again. Knowing that you died calmly does not help me at all to ease the profound grief I am feeling today. Even though it is only morning, today has ended for me.

Sunday, June 20

Where are you? My first morning — no James. I never realized that all of my morning routine centered around you. Everyone else is still sleeping. You and I always got up early. As I pour my coffee, I feel an urge to walk to the back door to open it for you. Looking into the cabinet I see the cereal boxes and your green box of dog biscuits. This morning is like no other. It is strangely the same as any other, but incomplete for me. I tell myself to just do what I've always done, so I sit in the family room to drink coffee and read. For the first time, I can't concentrate. Gazing around the room I see your picture on the wall, the standard poodle statue, your obedience ribbons. We had so many great times. You loved to go anywhere as long as you were with your human family. We need to visit grandparents because today is Father's Day. You will be missed by your dog "cousin," Sari, and all my family who know you are not coming with us today.

Monday, June 21

I have to go work today. Again, my morning is incomplete without you. How you filled my morning with your presence. You watched my every move and took your cues without a word. We knew each other so well, James. Could another dog ever know me so well? Good thing I have to work. Maybe I won't feel so bad. Should I talk about you at work? I might cry. People will understand if I do. They probably know what this is like.

Tuesday, June 22

I said that I would never get another dog when I learned of your diagnosis with lymphoma in April. Others said that I would change my mind, and I guess I knew I would. I feel the need to have you back and I know I can't. The only way I can get over this is to find a dog to love. I have some breeders to call. What should I do? I will think it over. I won't jump into anything.

Wednesday, June 23

The evenings and nights are still sad for me. I am going to make some calls to breeders. We have a lot of love to give to a dog. Because you were so wonderful, I want to have another like you. I know that all dogs have their own personality, so I know I will never have a dog exactly like you, but that's okay. You remember how I took so many pictures of you? Well, that's all I have now, pictures and the memories that I cherish. Actually, I have more. I have the experience of living with you for eight years. You made me into a "dog" person. I will always have a dog in my life until I can no longer care for one properly. You were my first and I will always love you.

Jean Marsch
Assistant Director, Human Resources
Green Bay, Wisconsin

JENNIFER'S CHAMPAGNE DELIGHT "CHAMMIE"

BUFF COCKER SPANIEL
15-YEAR-OLD FEMALE
SEPTEMBER 7, 1982 - MAY 6, 1998

Hello, My Sweet Girl,

It's your Momma, and I'm writing to tell you that I miss you more than ever. It has been one year exactly, since you crossed over the Rainbow Bridge. A lot has happened since then. I got married in September, but I'm sure you know that, as I know you're looking down on us, watching out for us.

Sometimes, when I see your picture, or remember something silly you used to do, I can't help but cry. You were such a BIG part of my life. My youth ended the day you left. I will always remember you Cham. People STILL talk about you...what a wonderful little girl you were ... You made a huge impact on people's lives. Everyone loved you.

Calleigh is doing fine. She misses you, but we are giving her lots of love. I think she misses her Momma licking her face more than anything. You always took such good care of her. She's getting older too, and someday soon, she'll cross the Bridge to be with you once again. I know you will be waiting for her.

Jarret put up some glow-in-the-dark stars on his bedroom ceiling, and he said to me the other night, "Momma, that star is going to be my Chammie star, because it's the biggest and the brightest!" He misses you too, so very much. I'm so glad he was old enough to know you before you passed.

Tomorrow, the one year anniversary of your death, I am going out to your grave at the pet cemetery, to plant Lilies of the Valley. I always visit you there...it brings me such peace just to be close to you. I love you so much, baby girl. Someday, we will be together again. However, until that time, I'll always keep you close in my heart. You were such a joy. I hope you are at peace, because you deserve nothing but that.

We love and miss you!
Momma, Daddy, Jarret, Calleigh (your daughter) and Sunny
x o x o x o x

Jennifer Flanik-Jarvis
Airline Employee
Hoffman Estates, Illinois

Besides love and sympathy,
animals exhibit other qualities connected
with the social instincts,
which in us would be called moral;
and I agree — that dogs possess something
very like a conscience.

—Charles Darwin

JESSE

LABRADOR/SHEPHERD MIX
1½-YEAR-OLD FEMALE
APRIL 1, 1997 - DECEMBER 28, 1998

Dear Jesse,

I know it has been a long time, but I wanted to tell you how much I love and miss you. All the things you did brightened our lives. You were the best dog ever. When I first saw you I fell in love. Even if I had known how many tears you would bring, I would still have brought you home. You were Dad's baby. You would sit on his lap even though you were fifty-five pounds. "Madame-Licks-A-Lot" he called you. You learned and we learned. You taught and we taught.

Why did you love us so much that you had to bite others to protect us? They were our friends, but you saw them as enemies. You loved us almost too much.

I am glad that I took you to the vet's with Dad. You were not even two years old yet. You still loved me in the end. As you lay on the table and the needle went in, you licked my face. It was if you were saying, "It's okay. I forgive you."

I love you. Please help our new puppy to adjust. I wish I could have held you for more of your life. Maybe then I would not be so sad. But as Rudyard Kipling so elegantly stated, "A short time loan is as bad as a long."

Marie Pierman
Student, age 13
Kettering, Ohio

JIN-JIN

MIXED BREED DOG
2-YEAR-OLD FEMALE
FEBRUARY 26, 1996 - DECEMBER 27, 1998

Jin-Jin,

The day you died was a wicked waste of beauty, of nature's form and loving grace, of recent motherhood, and loving companionship. If "beauty" ever had a name, it must have been called Jin-Jin.

If loving companionship is like a glittering crown, then you were its princess like Diana and the English Rose.

But above all, Jin-Jin, you loved and were loved. The day you died, it made the days cold and tears with anger unfold. If humankind is known to be our animals' deadliest enemy, then such an enemy is less likely to be, after being touched by one such little dog just like you. You made even the coldest person respect and love you overwhelmingly, no matter how cold they might be.

Even in your hours of little life left, you retained your magic to demand love and respect. You were magic itself!

Bless you Jin-Jin for having shared your life with me and me with you. Let me tell you, dear Spanky and Boy-Boy pine for you so sadly like I do. I have comforted them as they have comforted me, due to our joyless loss of you. And do remember, the echoes of our everlasting farewell will always be with you, my Sweet Jin-Jin.

I wasn't your master per se, I was your loving friend from the moment we met to the moment you died almost in my arms, my Sweet Jin-Jin. I reject the concept of master; no creature needs a master, but rather a loving friend that will always provide love, shelter and protection whenever, however, and wherever possible!!

Father Monty
Anglican Priest
Bay St. Louis, Mississippi

JOE

POODLE
19-YEAR-OLD MALE
JULY 12, 1979 - OCTOBER 19, 1998

To Joe, born a Dog and died a Friend,

I remember when you first came into my life and home. You were so small and cuddly with your tiny paws and soft fur. You were the runt of the litter and what some may have thought of as being timid, really was the nice and gentle disposition that you had.

As you got older you protected me by looking out the window and barking at everyone who walked by and attacking the mail as it came through the mail slot. When I had a tough day at work, you would be waiting for me with your tail wagging, just to say, "Welcome home. I missed you." You never had a bad day and I could always count on you to be there for me. Whenever I came home I could look up at the window in the back bedroom and you were there looking out and waiting.

When I sat down to read or watch T.V., you would hop up on my lap or lie down by my side, looking for attention. You never asked for anything more than to have me pat your head so you could go to sleep with your head on my leg. You never asked for anything, and the littlest things made you happy. Just a simple walk was great for you.

As you got older you moved around more slowly, your sight and hearing went. Then one day, old age finally took its toll and you couldn't stand on those old wobbly legs, but you waited for me to get home so we could say good-bye, and once I told you that it was okay, you went to a better place where you are young again.

In your almost twenty years you taught me about loyalty, unconditional love, forgiving and forgetting, and holding no grudges. Most of all you taught about doing because of love and not out of fear. There was no master/subject.

Joe, I miss you and I love you, and I know we will meet again.

Reason discovers the bridge between love for God and love for men — love for all creatures, reverence for all being, compassion with all life, however dissimilar to our own. Reverence for life comprises the whole ethic of love in its deepest and highest sense.

—Albert *Schweitzer*

Peace,
Alan

E. Alan Anstine
Probation Officer
Remington, Virginia

The language of friendship is not words, but meanings.
It is an intelligence above language.

—Henry David Thoreau

— Photo by Frank Spear

KILLER BOY

MINIATURE PINSCHER
5-YEAR-OLD MALE
FEBRUARY 1994 - MAY 17, 1999

Dear Killer Boy,

Hello son! I was hoping that I would not have to write this so soon. I know that it has only been a day since you crossed the Bridge, but we miss you so very much. It's hard to believe that you are gone when it seems like just yesterday that you were so healthy. I hope you understand the final decision we made for you yesterday, as it was breaking our hearts to see you suffer so much. It was as if you just gave up and felt like you had disappointed us, which could never happen.

We will both remember you as the spunky little guy that brought us both happiness and unconditional love every day that you were with us. It is so very hard to say goodbye to you as, to us, you were more than just a dog. You were our son.

I know that you are in a better place, and we want to make sure that you save us a spot for us when we get there so that we can be a family again. Remember that we loved you with all our hearts and souls. You will never be forgotten as you will live in our hearts forever.

With All Our Love,
Your Dads

P.S. You are missed by Grandma & Grandpa, Zeke, Sasha, Lobo, Kathy, Susan, and everybody whose heart you touched.

Kenneth Patten, Jr.
Phoenix, Arizona

KYLE VON HAMBSCH
"KYLE"

GERMAN SHORTHAIRED POINTER
11-YEAR-OLD MALE
APRIL 6, 1988 - FEBRUARY 1, 1999

Dear Kyle,

I write this letter to you not three feet from where you drew your last breath, sitting on the same yellow blanket that snuggled your body against the crisp winter morning. Roland's lying next to me. I can't believe it will be seven months tomorrow since you left. I hope you don't worry about us. It's just like I told you when I released you: we'll think about you every day, we'll miss you fiercely till the day we meet again, but we're okay. Mostly.

Sweet Kyle, you who had more nicknames than years, I wish you could tell me about the Rainbow Bridge. I want so desperately to believe in it. But you must be there, in the spirit world; heaven wouldn't be complete without dogs. Roland misses you, too. He's taken on some of your mannerisms: your snoring, the way you would recline on the patio, your back comfortably wedged against the side of the house as you lazily sniffed the breeze, the way you routinely knocked over the arm on the south side of the sofa. He still can't make elephant-cup ears the way you did, with your eyes half-closed, your whole body shimmying like a snake, so proud, so endearing.

We have all of your special prizes, especially the red prize, on the mantel with your ashes, your collar and leash and your picture.

It was so very hard to let you go, Kyle. So hard to know when it was time, until you could no longer do the things you loved, that made you a dog, that made you uniquely Kyle. Our last two hours together, outside with your head in my lap, I poured my heart out to you, trying not to convey my dread and overwhelming sadness, telling you how unutterably special to us you are and forever shall be, wrapping my love around you like a security blanket for a safe journey to the Bridge. So very hard. And every day I take Roland to the river to run and explore, I rue that you're not here to come along.

What love you took, you gave back a thousandfold. And your stories have taken on a life of their own. I can't single out one story as my favorite. They're all my favorites. Writing about you celebrates your life and keeps you close in my heart. You provided comfort and comedy whether you planned it or not. Which doesn't explain why I'm crying as I write this. Gone from my sight, but never from my heart.

Run and play, Buckethead. The part of your heart that was the strongest was the part science could never touch. That's the part I'll be bringing with me when we meet again.

I love you.

Tracy Landauer
Editor
Boise, Idaho

LACY

YELLOW LABRADOR RETRIEVER
9-YEAR-OLD FEMALE
DECEMBER 10, 1989 - NOVEMBER 15, 1998

Dear Lacy,

How I dream of you still, thinking of your beautiful blonde fur and soft brown eyes, gazing at me with endless love and understanding.

No matter what was going on in our lives, you were my best friend and always let me know it. In times of turmoil you refused to let me cry, and I would always end up laughing as you jumped on me to lick away my tears with such seriousness.

Oh, the times we both had, growing into adulthood together. Who would have known how much we would see and do? You were the one who would appreciate the joy of every outing with me in absolute silence, as we reveled in our companionship. Such mountains we climbed, you inspiring me all the way, even as you grew older.

It seems even as if fate looked kindly upon us for our last summer together, while I enjoyed two free months with you before I moved and began my new job. It wasn't until I was gone, before you could join me, that the cancer showed up. And it grew so quickly, my beautiful strong girl. Even as you laid nearly completely disabled within the month, your eyes shone bright through the pain, and you tried to play with your Frisbee and give me kisses the best you could. As unbearable as it was, we had to let you go, we could not let you continue to suffer. You even looked at me reassuringly as the vet began his work, and pleaded with your eyes for me not to cry; I know that you knew exactly what was happening.

I will never forget the strength and beauty in your last days, which never faltered from that of your whole life. I feel that you are my angel, my best friend, and I am infinitely grateful that I had the nine years with you that I did — as I know, the best years of my life. I look forward to holding you once again, in some other time and place.

Always Your Best Friend,
VLZ

Victoria Zinser
County Planner
Boynton Beach, Florida

The greatest pleasure of a dog
is that you may make a fool of yourself with him
and not only will he not scold you,
but he will make a fool of himself, too.

—Samuel Butler

LADY

BEAGLE/TERRIER MIX
15-YEAR-OLD FEMALE
APRIL 8, 1984 - APRIL 2, 1999

Dear Lady,

You were a companion to all of us. You were there for us through the pain and suffering of your later years. You struggled to get up when we called, and you painfully lay back down when we were fast asleep. We loved you for the fifteen years you spent with us. You touched the lives of not only our family, but also the neighbors, the relatives, even the vet and groomer. You were a wonderful dog, and we all miss you.

Laura Farrell
Student, age 17
Wilbraham, Massachusetts

LADY

AUSSIE/BLUE HEELER MIX
11-YEAR-OLD FEMALE
1983 - APRIL 9, 1994

Oh...my Lady,

What joy you have brought into my life. You, with those big brown eyes and that little stump of a tail, always wagging ... always smiling ... always so happy to see me. How can the years have passed so quickly that we have came to this day. It seems like only yesterday that you were running alongside my horse or beside me while I was jogging. You never needed a leash because you would never leave my side. My constant companion ... my best friend.

Now you are eleven ... much too young to be so sick. How can I say good-bye to you? How can I let you go? I am so sorry, girl, that I do not have a magic wand to cure you ... to help ease your pain. You were given to me free ... what a priceless gift I received.

How lucky for me that you came into my life and chose me to live out most of your years with. I wish we were at the beginning now, instead of the end. My tears fall on your soft gray fur, and you look at me...like you know. How will I survive without you? You have been there through all my tears ... my pain of losing Wayne ... my fear of the unknown. You were my protector ... my friend.. my comfort...in some of my deepest darkest hours you were there. You loved me unconditionally. You asked me for nothing and gave me so much. How do I say good-bye to someone who has given me such joy ... and asked so little in return?

So now, Lady, as the cancer eats away at that magnificent body of yours and pulls you away from my arms, I know the greatest gift that I can give to you is to let you go. How selfish a friend would I be to let you continue to suffer and not help you as you have helped me all these years.

It is not easy, girl, to say good-bye. Not easy to let you go. I know I must, yet how I pray for some miracle ... for some light to this darkness. So now I take you for one last car ride. This is an adventure I would rather not take with you. This time you do not sit tall in the seat like you were a human and not a dog. I can see your pain, and the tears will not stop flowing from my eyes.

It is time now ... and as I hold you in my arms and tell you that it is okay, I want you to know that I will always love you. You forever will be in my heart and a part of my soul. I know now that God only gave me my angel Lady for a short time. I will never forget you. And as the doctor gives you that medicine that I know will end your pain ... it is like ... he gave me a shot ... that has started mine.

Good-bye, my sweet little angel ... wait for me at Rainbow Bridge ... and know always that there has been no greater gift given to me than you.

Pat Wohrley
Registered Nurse
Wichita, Kansas

LUCKY

BORDER COLLIE MIX
11-YEAR-OLD FEMALE
1988 - APRIL 22, 1999

Lucky, Lucky, Lucky,

Oh, how I ache knowing I will never say your name again. That I will never know your sweet kisses, your loving voice.

The birds are out again, the grass is growing and the trees are all in flower, Lucky. You are about to miss your first summer — how dare the world go on without you.

I am so sorry for anything I did or didn't do to prevent your death, I know how much you loved life. Your passing is so unexpected it takes my breath away.

The pain has slowly receded to a dull nagging, a feeling that something is missing, something isn't right. I'm shocked to see my slippers in the same place on the floor in the morning. You used to steal and hide them every time. I was cooking the other night and dropped a piece of shrimp, again surprised that you weren't there to swoop it up.

You meant so much to me, girl, you stuck by me for the best and worst times of my life. You were always there to be counted on.

I know the years will go by and there will be other companions, but you were the one and only. I will never forget you. You were a gift from God, and I can feel you waiting for me. Wait patiently, my pretty girl, for one day we will be together again.

Love,
Mommy

Jennifer Allard
Advertising Sales Representative
Saunderstown, Rhode Island

Dogs' lives are too short...
their only fault, really.

—Agnes Sligh Turnbull

LUCY

COCKER SPANIEL
5-YEAR-9-MONTH-OLD FEMALE
APRIL 18, 1983 - JANUARY 12, 1999

My Dear Little Lucy,

You have been gone for almost four months now, and not a day goes by that I don't think of you. You were, and always will be, the love of my life. I miss you so much and wish that I could hold you once again, and tell you how much I love you. I miss all of the things that you used to do to cheer me up when I was having a bad day, because no matter what the day would bring, you'd always put sunshine back into it. I miss seeing your little tail wagging fiercely when I came home. I miss you always being at my side, no matter where I was. I miss seeing you hanging out the window of the car when we would go "bye byes," your tongue hanging out, with that happy look on your face.

But I know that you're in Heaven now, with God, and the cat. And I know that you are listening when I talk to you every day, and although I cannot see you now, I know that you walk beside me once again.

My dear sweet little girl, you will always live on in my heart and soul. No one will ever replace you, and I will never ever forget you. I know that you are well once again. It was so sad to see you slowly fade a little more each and every day. I prayed every night for a miracle for you. But even though it never came, you refused to give up the will to live. I only wish that I could sometimes be as strong as you were. You were a true inspiration to us all. I will love you forever.

Your Daddy,
Mike

Mike Kucharik
Shipping Manager
Stowe, Pennsylvania

MEGAN

SHEPHERD/TERRIER
6-YEAR-OLD FEMALE
MARCH 3, 1991 - APRIL 17, 1997

Megan, my Sweet Baby Girl,

The days pass, things still go on, but my thoughts of you are an every day occurrence. You are so deeply embedded in my heart. How can I forget you. You were the reason for my happiness. You were the sunshine in my life and the stars in the sky.

Your innocence touched me in a way that words just simply cannot express. Those eyes that melted my very soul, how I miss them. How I miss you, my little love. The summer days are soon to be here once again. Our favorite time! As we shared precious moments just before the sun went down. The quiet of the day as we watched the birds eat their supper I left each night. I would lie on the lounge chair and you would be on my lap feeling so safe and contented. Why did you let me love you so, for you to be taken from me at only six years old?

I hold on to this place called the Rainbow Bridge. I need to believe that you are there happy and playing and that you are a special little angel. Will I ever see you again Meg? For the thought of never gazing my eyes upon your sweetness is too much to bear. I will always love you, my sweet baby girl.

Walk with the angels, my love, my life!

Paula Johnson
Homemaker
Staten Island, New York

MOPSIE

COCKER SPANIEL, BLACK AND TAN
13-YEAR-OLD FEMALE
JUNE 9, 1986 - MARCH 19, 1999

Dear Mopsie:

I miss you, my little girl. You were so much a part of my life that without you I feel a part of me died also that night. I know you are waiting for me at Rainbow Bridge and we will be together once again. In the meantime I am trying to survive without you in my arms or on my lap.

The decision to have you put to sleep is probably the hardest thing I have ever had to do, and I realize I probably made you suffer for a while, while I made that dreadful decision. But you never made a sound like you were hurting. That was the way you were; always putting me first and caring about my feelings. You always knew my mood and tried to comfort me when I was sad, or jumped and wiggled when I was happy.

You will always be my "star"; my leading lady. Always remember how much you were loved and how much you are missed. I learned unconditional love from you, courage, and trust. I am glad that you stole my heart when I saw you. Your kitty companions miss you also. I have an angel doggie that looks exactly like you, and I know that you have wings and a halo just like this little statue because you were an angel in this life.

My precious little girl, play with your friends at the Bridge and be patient. We will be united again one day and be together forever. I know you lived longer than we expected because you knew you had to prepare me for your leaving. Your will to live was greater than the universe, and I'll always be grateful for that. Please know that you will always be in my heart, and memories will always flood my mind. You are only a heartbeat away but, oh how I yearn to touch you, love you, and get your kisses. You were my strength in times of sorrow, my joy in times of happiness. Now I have to find ways to go on without that.

Bubba, the cat, sleeps in your bed and has taken over where you left off. She meets me at the basement door, rolls over for her belly to be scratched, sits up and begs for food. All the things you used to do. But somehow it is different. Nothing can take your place. I have written this letter with many tears flowing but with each tear, I try to find some healing. Never to forget, but just to ease the pain. I know you are not sorrowing because where you are there is just happiness and joy. I am going to say goodbye now, my precious little girl, until we see each other again.

Love,
Mom

Darlene Kesner
Medical Transcriptionist
Bellevue, Nebraska

You think dogs will not be in heaven?
I tell you, they will be there long before any of us.

—Robert Louis Stevenson

MUFFIE

WESTIE
6-YEAR-OLD FEMALE
OCTOBER 12, 1990 - OCTOBER 17, 1996

Muffie, my Sweet Little Girl,

You were with us such a short time. It has been over two years now and my heart is still heavy. You were so bright. You knew what we were saying to you, sometimes before we even said it.

Oh how you loved to go on trips. You would sit in your special place, maybe rest your head on Daddy's lap or climb on my lap to get a better view of the world. You had so much love to give.

When you got sick everything happened so fast. One minute you were fine and the next you're gone. Just three days!!

I didn't think we would ever get over the pain. There isn't a day that goes by that I don't think of you. We now have two more Westie girls, and though they can't fill your little paws, they have filled a big hole in my heart. I hope you found old Reggie boy at the Bridge and you two are having a dog-gone good time. Someday we will all meet again.

Muffie, my sweet girl, I miss you so much.

Terrie Bahndorf
Homemaker
Cedar Rapids, Iowa

MUFFIN

TOY POODLE, WHITE
15-YEAR-OLD FEMALE
JANUARY 1984 - MAY 2, 1999

My Dear Little Baby,

Well, it's been four very lonely and long weeks, but fifteen very short years. I'll never forget the day I brought you home. It was two months before high school graduation. My friend had asked me if I wanted the puppy I had seen at her house because her stepfather was abusing it. I brought you home. We already had one dog. Remember Inky? My parents said NO WAY!!! But when I started crying and said "but she was abused" and told them the story they changed their tune. I named you Muffin. I came home between classes to feed you and let you out. We went through so much that year. Every time my boyfriend and I broke up you would be right there kissing my face and licking my tears away.

Three years later, in 1987, I married someone else. We went to get you a new playmate — Cheeta, remember? She loved you right from the start. She was so tiny, that's how Chihuahuas are, that she wanted to sleep with you wherever you were. She even slept with you the last night you were with us. She really misses you.

Two years later I got our third furbaby, Blackie, another abused dog that I felt sorry for because he was born without eyes. Your father at the time said if I brought him home, we were through. Needless to say, we divorced a few months later. I met your new daddy right away. He was so good to all of you. He took care of the three of you like he had been doing it forever. In March of 1992 we brought home another future playmate for you. Our little Amanda. When I was in the hospital giving birth, the picture of my three furbabies was my focal point. Then in May of 1994 we brought home Alison, another little girl. In 1996 I suffered a miscarriage and you were right by my side the whole recovery, kissing away my tears like usual. What would I have done without you? What WILL I do without you? In January of 1998 we brought home our third daughter, Abby. Remember her? You were starting to show signs of old age by then.

On Saturday, May 1, as you fell into your water dish that morning trying to get a drink, I started crying. That day, as you lay in your bed, I sat by you and told you to please show me a sign that it was OK to put you to sleep. That night at supper time was the first time ever that you didn't come to your plate. Daddy and I tried everything to get you to eat. We even tried to give you water through a syringe. I knew right then that you were giving me "your" sign. We made you comfortable for the night, and I prayed to God that you would pass in your sleep. Needless to say you were still hanging on the next morning. We called the vet, and sure enough, your body was shutting down, and it was time. Daddy and I held you to the end. I had my face buried in yours as the vet inserted the needle in your hind leg. You didn't flinch. I just told you how much I loved you and I was so sorry.

We brought you home and buried you right outside my bedroom window. Amanda and Alison drew pictures on your coffin and wrote they love you. All of us kissed you goodbye before we closed the lid. We even let Blackie and Cheeta say their goodbyes too.

Mother's Day was really hard, baby. That's the day I always planted flowers and you would ALWAYS lay alongside of me as I was doing it. I forced myself to do it in memory of you. Come October when we bring our 4th and final baby home, it will be so hard, because I will be waiting for your greeting as I walk through the door with your new baby. You will be forever loved and always missed. Love you, baby!

Mommy, Daddy and Girls

Beth Coutre'
Peru, Illinois

NEGRITA

CHIHUAHUA MIX
17-YEAR-OLD FEMALE
UNKNOWN - APRIL 24, 1996

Negrita,

How to write to you? You have been gone since April 24, 1996, but certainly have not been away from our thoughts — in those you are with us every day.

You just appeared in the garage. Someone had dumped you, we are certain because the country road is too far from anywhere to have come on your own. Suddenly there was a little black frightened creature under the car.

We called you Negrita J. Snarl, often Snarl for short, because you loved people, but didn't especially like other dogs, often curling your lip and snarling at the others — pint size creature that you were. Before long you were a country-city dog, traveling with us back and forth from farm to city and taking over my little yellow Volky as yours.

You were unconditional love, small enough to almost fit in a pocket, with huge ears way out of proportion for your tiny face. You were so intelligent, so quick to respond to any comment, so delighted to be part of any activity.

I remember in the city we would go out to dinner at the small place of a wonderful Jamaican chef who would prepare chicken just for you. Not as in some European places where dogs are allowed in restaurants, in San Juan you would quietly and secretly stay under the table and have your dinner as we had ours.

Negrita. We loved you. You were a special little character, and you'll always live on with us.

Mary Ann Davies
Utuado, Puerto Rico

What dogs?!
These are my children, little people with fur
who make my heart open a little wider.

—Oprah Winfrey

NIKKI

BOUVIER DES FLAUNDRES
9-YEAR-OLD FEMALE
JANUARY 11, 1990 - MAY 26, 1999

My Darling Nikki,

It seems like a cruel joke that God would allow me to experience unconditional love and devotion, just to take it away. That is what has happened with your death. I am grateful that I was allowed to be with you nine wonderful years. My heart is breaking. Our home is empty — all because you are no longer with me. I cannot bear to put your food dish away. If I do, I will be admitting that you are not coming back, and I am not ready for that.

I can still see you hopping up and down as I fix your dinner. That was quite a feat for a 110-lb. dog. I can still see you chasing the birds in the park. Well, actually it was their shadows. You never did figure out that there was a bird over your head making that shadow. You were so sweet and gentle that you couldn't imagine anyone being afraid of you. You loved human babies and kittens. You would have made a wonderful mother, but that wasn't possible with your hip dysplasia. You were so strong and endured so much pain. I was so proud to be your mommy.

You depended on me, and I let you down. Please forgive me. If I could have saved you, I would have. I tried so hard to find a way to keep you with me because I needed you more than you needed me. Everyone said I shouldn't let you suffer. I pray that you were letting me know that it was time for you to pass on. I know you were tired of the pain, the pills and injections, and the vet exams. Now you can be with Duchess, my first baby. You can keep each other from being lonely. I have been blessed with the chance to be a part of your life, just as I was with Duchess. I tried to be worthy of your love.

Sleep well my darlings. I miss you.

George Anne Brown
Social Worker
Memphis, Tennessee

NIKKI

TOY POODLE
10-YEAR-OLD MALE
1989 - FEBRUARY 26, 1999

I will remember the night we met, when I was taking the big guys, Buddy and Sissy, out for a walk. You ran up to me and your eyes said, "Help me." I picked you up. You were so thin and battered.

I will remember bringing you home from the veterinarian after your surgery to save your life. They fixed your fractured jaw. You came home with only two teeth, one-third of your jaw bone, and a crooked mouth, which made you look like a "wise guy." You were a bundle of energy, pain free, and what an appetite!

I will remember when I would get your sweater and you would jump on the couch and get so excited, it was hard to put it on you because you knew you were going out with the big guys.

I will remember when I took you to the store and you would look around so proudly and seem to say, "Look at me. Aren't I special and beautiful?"

I will remember when you collapsed, and I rushed you to the doctor. We thought you were going to recover.

I will remember bringing you home after three days. You were very weak, but mentally you were my Nikki. The next day I knew you were just too tired, and I know now you came home to say good-bye. Hey Nik, I have your memorial stone in the garden where you loved to lay and look around.

I will remember the last time I held you in my arms. I miss you so. Forever in my heart.

Judy Goldman
Antioch, California

P. J.

CHIHUAHUA
12-YEAR-OLD FEMALE
JULY 22, 1985 - JULY 3, 1998

To my Dearest P.J.,

As I sit here tonight with Bam Bam at my feet playing with B.B., thinking of all the love we had for you, it brings tears to my eyes. I still cannot think about you without crying. The pain of losing you is just sometimes more than I can hardly bear. I miss you sitting on the coffee table watching the door waiting for me to come in the house. The yelps of joy you had for me. I miss you laying at my pillow at night always close to me.

I remember the first time I saw you. You came to me on Sherrie's fifteenth birthday. You were so tiny and loving. You loved everyone, but we had something together from the first. A bond of some kind I cannot explain. I remember the day you were spayed. I would not let the vet keep you overnight. I slept with you on the floor all night, afraid you would fall off the bed.

I remember the Christmas I had your picture taken with Santa Claus. At first he kind of thought I was crazy, but they did it. I have the picture framed, and even now I stop and look at you. I still have all the pigs I collected over the years because they reminded me of you. You were always a little overweight.

Looking back, I can see the years were taking a toll on you. More and more, you were not feeling well enough to come and greet me. Instead of walking out the door, you waited for me to carry you out. No more than I would want someone to take away my dignity, I couldn't take away yours. I know you forgive me...I just can't seem to forgive myself. I remember our last day together as I bathed you and talked to you, telling you how much I loved you. You laid in my arms, loving me back.

I will always remember the last look you gave me at the vet's office. You also had tears in your eyes as I know you were saying goodbye. I remember after they took you, I cried for them to stop, to bring you back, that I changed my mind, Sherrie and I in each other's arms, sharing the pain, the pain that is still with me, and I don't know if it will ever go away.

I can picture you in my mind in the yard hopping through the grass, and surely you are somewhere doing that right now. I believe in God and the hereafter, and as I believe that one day I will see my mother, father, and all my loved ones gone ahead, and that you, P.J., will greet me with that yelp of joy that only you could make.

Dorothy Williamson
Accounting Clerk
Houston, Texas

God evidently does not intend us all to be rich,
or powerful, or great,
but he does intend us all to be friends.

—Ralph Waldo Emerson

— Photo by Frank Spear

PANAMA
"MAMA'S GIRL"

CHOW/PITBULL MIX
13-YEAR-OLD FEMALE
1983 - SEPTEMBER 1997

Dear Girl,

I miss you so much and think of you often. I know you are still around in spirit. Every now and then I hear the creak of your old hips. I still see your shadow every once in a while. I miss those big brown eyes smiling up at me. I especially miss those tender moments when you would "spoon" up next to me on the bed and tilt your head back to give me gentle licks. I will treasure those times always.

The boy is getting old now too. He will be joining you soon, and I know you will show him the ropes and take care of him until I get there. You two can wrestle like you used to. I miss you, girl, and even though I know there will be other dogs in my life, you will always be "mama's girl" in my heart.

I'll love you forever and until we meet again....

Kim Kincaid
El Paso, Texas

PARIS

TRI-COLOUR SHELTIE MIX
14½-YEAR-OLD FEMALE
FEBRUARY 14, 1985 - JUNE 22, 1999

My Dearest Darling, Paris,

From the moment I first laid eyes on you — a mischievous, very bright, chubby and adorable puppy — my heart has been yours. And I gave it to you gladly, for the joy you gave me back was beyond belief.

On that first day I saw you, we had a special connection. Yet even then I could never have imagined the adventures and fun we would have together, the games we would invent together, the travels we would take together. Every moment I've spent with you has been pure, unadulterated joy.

And now, my darling, it's time for you to go on a journey without me. I am so sad at the thought of a life without you that my heart feels like it will break in pieces. But I promised you that I would always be there when you needed me, and now, when you need me most of all, I cannot let you down.

So go, my darling — leave your pain and illness behind — go to where your daddy, Blair, is waiting for you with open arms. It is the final act of love that I can do for you. I only ask that you remember me now and then, while you're happily chasing balls and squirrels in heaven — for not a second of a day will go by when I won't be thinking of you and missing you, my precious and beautiful girl.

Go gently — we send you with love.

Jan Johnson
Retailer
Kelowna, B.C. Canada

PEPSI COLA

COCKAPOO
19-YEAR-OLD FEMALE
OCTOBER 30, 1981 - JUNE 13, 1999

To Pepsi,

I miss you, little one. How very much I ache for your presence here beside me. I feel so hollow... so empty. The place you shared is burned with pain. I called you "just a dog" and tried to remember that. It didn't work. You were more than "just a dog." You were my constant companion of nineteen years. Always by my side or in my lap. You always knew when to listen and when to speak. Your eyes told me untold depths of understanding and love. You were my #1 dog of life. Another can never replace you. Years may come and go, perhaps even other dogs, but you remain. You, little Pepsi. My hug-a-pup, my love in good times and bad. "Just a dog," they say. Oh, but what a dog! Pepsi...

Barb Redmond
Mason, Michigan

All knowledge, the totality of all questions and answers,
is contained in the dog.

—Franz Kafka

PONCE

AKITA/CHOW MIX
6½-YEAR-OLD MALE
UNKNOWN - MAY 14, 1998

Dear Ponce:

As I sit here crying, I can't help but wonder why you had to leave me so soon.

You were my dear friend, my best friend, and I loved you so much. You were always there for me when no one else was. When I had a bad day at work, I knew I would come home and find you greeting me at the garage door. When I drove into the driveway, I knew your beautiful face would be looking out the window, tail wagging because I'd arrived home. You were my protector, Ponce, and I never felt frightened when you were around because you had that scary look, but in reality you were a scared big guy who just looked intimidating, backing off from strangers all the while barking that loud, vicious sounding bark.

I miss you so much, Ponce, that I wonder how I get up each morning and begin my day without you by my side. I hope that one day I will see you again. Until that day, Ponce, please know how much I loved you (and always will) and how I miss you, and if I had to give everything else up to have you back, I would.

It's coming up on a year since you left this world, Ponce, and I dread the anniversary of your departure. I think about you all the time, and I cry for you often. I hope you are happy, and I look forward to seeing you again someday. I love you, big boy and I will NEVER forget you!

Barbara

Barbara C.
Albuquerque, New Mexico

REX

SHEPHERD/LABRADOR
8-MONTH-OLD MALE
DECEMBER 1998 - AUGUST 28, 1999

Dear Rex,

How quickly life changes. I'm so sorry for not training you better. I let you run free because you loved it so. When that car hit you and killed you, something in me died too. Rex, I have never been so adored by anyone as I was by you. You were a treasure. More human than most people I know. And smart as a whip. I hope you're chasing shadows and playing ball and munching on a pig's ear (DON'T BURY IT...ENJOY IT!!!) You're in God's great hands now. I pray He takes good care of you until mommy joins you some day.

I Love You, Boy. Thank You For Loving Me.

God bless you,
Mommy

Rhonda Nave
Housecleaning Service
Hayward, California

RINGO

GERMAN SHEPHERD
13-YEAR-OLD MALE
MARCH 4, 1984 - NOVEMBER 1997

Ringo ...

Today I found your ball. The big football made of leather patches. The minute I saw it, I also saw your sparkling, eager eyes, the way they looked when we played tug-of-war with it. You would pull me clear across the room, my big, strong, German Shepherd boy! I found the ball when I was cleaning out the room we slept in the last couple of years. I moved my bed downstairs when your hind legs got weak and the stairs became a problem for you. Leaving you downstairs by yourself was out of the question. And as you and I know, you were the only male ever forgiven for snoring in my bedroom!

Your first day in our home. You walked in and fell instantly in love. Not with any of the humans, but with Tootsie. The cat. Love at first sight on your part! Tootsie had a bit more dignity, but as the friendly creature she was, she took it upon herself to help raise you. The fact that you soon grew to be about twenty times her size, never bothered her. She was the boss, and you both knew it. She was also your patient friend, who showed you how to behave around cats, how to scratch their backs. Cats have shared your bed and licked you and stolen chunks of meat out of your mouth. Kittens have climbed into your food bowl to eat your food, and you never bit them.

From that first day, till the day I had to take you on your last ride in the car, you filled my life with love and companionship. You also kept the shoe repairman in business, kept unwanted company out of the house, stole the Christmas dinner more than once, left scratch marks on the table where you would sit and look out of the window when you had to be alone. I never moved that table, but put a blanket on top of it when I left the house. The scratch marks from your claws will probably never be removed. Who cares if others think they look bad?

You and the cats had fun alone in the house, always very inventive as far as entertainment goes. Like the way you cooperated about the garbage. You opened the door and got the bucket out of the closet. Together you spread the contents carefully around the house, kitchen, livingroom, hall, and helped each other sort out any good stuff that stupid humans accidentally had thrown in the garbage and wasted.

How you loved to surprise me! And what better surprise than half a loaf of bread (mysteriously disappeared from the kitchen the same day) under my pillow? A night snack? Last winter I burned the last of the logs you insisted on carrying home from our walks in the woods. Big or small ones, some of them really heavy. The logs were your prey that you proudly carried home and put in your very own stack outside. I thanked all good spirits you had no other hunting instincts. Logs and sticks and balls and snowballs; those were your prey.

I didn't love you any more than my other dogs, but saying goodbye was a lot harder with you. The others died naturally when it was time. With you, I had to decide when, how and where you would be going on your way to the Rainbow Bridge. That almost broke my heart and my spirit. My life had been very hard sometimes, but that is truly the most terrible experience I've ever had. Worst of all was that I didn't feel it was time yet. Parts of your body weren't working as well as they used to, but you were still playful and happy and you loved riding in the car. You were curious and enjoyed life.

And I had no choice.

It was done in the best and kindest way for you. You fell asleep munching your favorite snack, while we hugged and cuddled, and you didn't even bother to look at the vet who gave you that final shot. You didn't suffer, but I did. I didn't think I would ever get over it. Then you came to me in a dream. I realized that I was the only one who could see you. You were there for me only. It filled me with sadness, but it was a good kind of sadness. I came to peace with the fact that you had come to say goodbye and that you would not be here with me anymore, not in this life. You were OK.

I don't know what happened that night, if it was my own subconscious that tried to comfort me, or if it was your spirit that helped me when I was so unhappy. But that dream helped me say goodbye and to be able to treasure the good memories. Now I imagine you playing with the other dogs and cats who have left us, and maybe with my father, who was such a dog-lover and who you spent a lot of time with.

And maybe you have a ball to play tug-of-war with...

Loving you forever,
Your pal and Mamma,
Bjørg

Bjørg Rygnestad
Welding Inspector/Non-Destructive Test (NDT) Technician
Mandal, Norway

One touch of nature makes the whole world kin.

—William Shakespeare

— Photo by Frank Spear

RONTU

KEESHOND
7-YEAR-OLD FEMALE
NOVEMBER 11, 1990 - DECEMBER 27, 1997

What could I give you in return, my sweet dog,
for the years you guarded me from solitude?
And for the joy which leaped on me every time
I was benumbed by the sterile void in me?
Like a poet you are seldom recognized
For your silent vigilance of predators.
You have no tears, yet I heard your inner sobs
When your sister left us behind suddenly.
And you do laugh even at me, yes you do,
Perhaps thinking your old man would never guess.
And when you see the can of beef in my hand
You frisk as if I shall give you the whole world.
Yet in my skin I still carry the needles
Impaled in me by those to whom I gave more.
O, my sweet dog, sit beside me and tell me,
Why should you cross our last river without me?

Terri Bricker
Author and Rescue League Missionary
Pittsburgh, Pennsylvania

RUFFIE

MIXED BREED
14½-YEAR-OLD MALE
JULY 10, 1984 - JANUARY 22, 1999

Ruffie,

I remember when we got you from the pound that day. So small and quiet you stayed in the back of the kennel. The others jumped and played, but not you. You were so small and scared.

I remember that day it snowed in Tennessee. The first time you had seen it fall. What a wonder. You looked so amazed till I opened the door and called your name. Then you ran so fast into the house, and you stayed next to the wood stove staying warm.

I remember when we stopped at Four Corners. You sat in four states at one time. Colorado, Utah, New Mexico, and Arizona. What a picture that was. I remember how you chased ground squirrels in California. If you had caught one, you would not have known what to do. But oh, how you loved to chase them. I remember after we moved to Florida. You did not understand why squirrels here ran up trees instead. They were not as much fun to chase. But still you chased them.

I remember how you loved to play with your tennis ball. You caught it every time. You would bring it back, then we would play tug-of-war. When you tired, you would place the ball between your paws. You would guard it from us.

I remember how you would follow me from fish tank to fish tank to make sure I fed them all. Then off to bed we would head. Between Mom and me you slept, or on my pillow. I remember how you stayed by us. Anytime we were sick, you were always there. Right next to us, giving us love, making us feel better.

I remember how you waited for your morning walk. No matter how long it took for me to wake up.

I remember the day the vet said cancer. That we had only weeks, maybe months. That I would know when. That I would have to choose.

I remember that day. We awoke. We walked. We went for a ride. We stopped for lunch. You reached the end. To the vet we rushed. It was time. But it had only been sixteen days.

I remember how Brandy cried. Mom rushed from work. We said good-bye. I held you and kissed you. The vet helped you on your way. I cried so much.

I remember the things we did. The time we had. And now that is all I can do. No longer can I hold you. No longer can I touch you. No longer can I see you. But I can feel you near. I wait till we are together again. Till I can hold you. Till I can touch you. Till I can see you.

Ruffie, I hope you are happy. I miss you so much. I hope you are at a place I can find. I want to be with you, but it is not my time. Please forgive me because I am sad. Please forgive me because I cry. You were my joy, my boy, the friend, the buddy, the pal that everyone wishes they had. I still see you and feel you, too.

I wish I could hold you some more. I will follow you one day, then together we will stay. My eyes, they hurt, my nose is raw, my heart is heavy. But someday, my friend, we will be together, and then there will be no pain. Be not sad for me. Run and play. Be free, my pal. Then I pray that "you and me," will be "we." My buddy, my pal, my friend, good-bye.

Mike

William M. Jenkins
Retired United States Marine
Jacksonville, Florida

RUPERT

ROTTWEILER/NEWFOUNDLAND/MASTIFF
3½-YEAR-OLD MALE
DECEMBER 12, 1994 - JUNE 29, 1998

To Rupert, my big black furry protector,

You walked side by side with me for miles feeling my pain, confusion and struggles. Throughout a time where my childhood fears chased me and haunted me, you protected me.

I wish you could have stayed longer, but your pain caught up with you so soon. Our walks were shortened but always faithful, you watched over my sleep. You were my friend that could hear all those horrors and never judge me. You only loved me.

I miss you in many ways. I think of our last ride together and holding your big, beautiful head in my arms as you took your last breath. I feel your spirit. You are still my protector and a part of my soul.

As always, love,
Vickie

Vickie L. Smith
Homeless Outreach Worker
Cleveland, Ohio

No one appreciates
the very special genius of your conversation
as much as the dog does.

—Christopher Morley

RUSTY

RED DOBERMAN
10-YEAR-OLD FEMALE
OCTOBER 13, 1988 - AUGUST 13, 1998

Dear Little Girl,

We miss you and wish you were here again.

I used to get impatient when you would want to sit with your head on my lap or press up against me when I was standing or walking, but I would love to have you here to do that again. We have you in the little crypt here near the house on the top of our hill overlooking the big valley where you used to sit and watch the cars come and go down on the road below. You truly watched our place and gave warning of everything you saw.

We have decided that you are the only red Dobie that we will ever have. I hope you are with your mother, Sheena, and are running races like you used to, seeing who would beat who to the pipe under the road to see if the rabbit was still there. You might have been the runt of the litter, but your bravery and orneriness made up for your small size.

We have your pictures above our desks and hope that you are wandering around visiting us and watching out for us. Bear, the Rottweiler mix, missed you when you left us. She sat so close to where we laid you to rest. She still looks out over the valley, and when the Shirley's dogs are let outside, she runs to bark and say hi. She doesn't have any company anymore.

Bye for now. I know there is a better place for you where you are.

Mom and Dad

Lorraine Thomas
Owner, K&L Cactus and Succulent Nursery
Ione, California

SANTINI

GOLDEN RETRIEVER
15-YEAR-OLD MALE
FEBRUARY 27, 1984 - NOT YET

Well, Santini,

You're still the shining star, even at fifteen. When I brought you home a long time ago, I knew that we would be lifelong friends. I have so many things that I want to tell you, even though I really know that you know how much I love you.

You have been my highs when I was low. You have always been there for me and with me. You felt my pain and shared my joys. When I brought home the twins after they were born you were right there at their side. Loving and kissing them like they were yours. You stood guard, you watched the house, and got all excited when Stevie came home. You even got excited when you had to get the newspaper and bring it into the house. You never had a bad moment. If angels look like you then you are my angel.

I have your little pup now. At least I will have some of you when you decide to go. I know that the time is close. Your breathing is so heavy, and you have such a hard time getting up and sitting down. I try to be there for you to help you up, but I know that it's hard. You amaze me! I cannot believe that you still walk across the rocks to get the newspaper. We have so much property here, and I know that it takes all of you to do this for me. I could never take that from you.

I know when you feel that it is time for you to go that you will somehow show me the strength to let go. I will be here right by your side when the time comes.

I just wanted to say thank you for being a part of our family. I know that you have had a wonderful life, and I will love you always. My angel, I will see you in heaven.

We love you, Santini,
Suzi, Steve, Brooke, Nichole and Anthony

Suzi Annunziata
Fitness Instructor
West Palm Beach, Florida

Note: Santini passed on June 2, 1999, a little more than a month after this was written. He will be greatly missed.

SARA

QUEENSLAND HEELER/BLACK LABRADOR
12-YEAR-OLD FEMALE
FEBRUARY 1987 - MAY 12, 1999

Dearest Sara,

When we took you to the vet today, it was only to find out what was wrong. We knew if it was serious (which the doctor prepared us for) that we would make the decision to help you pass and would be by your side.

We are so upset that we were too late. Your doctor called us and said you were dying. We rushed over there, but you'd already passed. I hurt so much inside because I never would have let you go through that by yourself. You were always a very unselfish little dog, taking a back seat to others, and now when you needed me the most I wasn't there. I love you so much, my little pod puppy (you always loved cuddling into your oval foam bed) and I hope you'll forgive me for not getting there soon enough. I hope your journey was not painful and that you knew in your heart I love you. I will miss you terribly tonight and for the rest of my life.

Mommy

Pam Hanna
Product Specialist
Pleasanton, California

Man must understand his universe
in order to understand his destiny.

—Neil Armstrong

SEGER

GERMAN SHEPHERD
12-YEAR-OLD MALE
AUGUST 1985 - SEPTEMBER 3, 1997

Dear Seger,

Even after all this time, I still miss you so much. You were such a handsome Shepherd with big brown eyes that seemed to say so much. You were such a big, gentle friend. You weren't just a pet, but our protector, companion, and playmate to Michelle, Nicole and Derek.

You were always a faithful friend who kept me company through my three pregnancies while my husband, Kevin, worked the night shift. With you there beside me I never felt alone. You made me laugh with your big bunny ears and the way your head tilted when we spoke to you.

The time came when we had to make a heart wrenching decision to put you to sleep. You were struggling just to get up and walk. The night before you died we invited your favorite family and friends over to say good-bye to you. The next morning we took you to the vet and stayed with you. We told you what a good dog you were and how much we loved you. You looked so peaceful as you quietly slipped away. We hope you know that you fulfilled your purpose on this earth and that we will always love you.

The hardest part was coming home and opening the door, and that sad, empty moment when we realized you were not there to greet us. Sometimes I still expect to see you there.

We will never forget you, Seger.

Susan O'Rourke
Customer Service Representative
Cambridge, Massachusetts

SHADOW

BLACK LABRADOR
12-YEAR-OLD FEMALE
OCTOBER 1, 1985 - OCTOBER 3, 1997

Shadow,
   The earth began to move today, as I thought of you
   Your life has been so long and full, good for me and you
   You will always live in my heart, never will I fear
   You've been the best friend I could have, all through the years
   You have been a good friend to me
   You have been a good friend to me
   The dawn is quickly coming now, the sun is almost up
   The leaves are softly blowin' now, blowin' down the road
   Crowley in the distance shines in the morning sun
   Your life has been so long and full, always on the run
   You have been a good friend to me
   You have been a good friend to me
   Life is so mysterious, sometimes you never know
   Why some may live and some may die, why teardrops fall
   Sometimes there's no reason for the things that happen here
   You have to tell the ones you love, that they are so dear
   And you have been a good friend to me
   You have been a good friend to me
   SHADOW you have been a good friend to me

Tom Schemenauer
Financial Planner / Songwriter
Mammoth Lakes, California

SPUNKIE ROCCO

POODLE
14-YEAR-OLD MALE
AUGUST 15, 1985 - JUNE 25, 1998

Dear Spunk,

Oh, my baby boy, how miss you. I still can't believe that you have been at the Bridge for eleven months. For the last eleven months, I have felt you inside of me … in my heart and my soul. I used to tell you all the time that our bond could never be broken and it looks like Mommy was right. I know you're watching over me and guiding me.

You lived such a full life. We lived our lives for each other. It was always you and me, baby. I still feel like it is you and me. Everything I do, Spunk, I still do it for you. I find myself saying, what would Spunky want me to do? Somehow the answer always comes to me. It's you answering me, isn't it baby?

I learned so much from you. You were so strong and so tough. You were so little, but had the biggest heart in the world. I'm trying to live up to you, baby. And trying to make you proud of me the way I was soooooo proud of you.

I'll never forget when you were only four years old and you got so sick. They told me you were not going to make it. Well, you shocked everyone. The vets said there was no medical reason for you have pulled through. They said you had to have done it out of love. You did for me, baby. You did it for your Mommy. I had you for ten more years. Every day was a gift from God, Himself. I never got mad at God for taking you from me. He needed you with him. I don't know why, but someday I will find out.

I always told everyone that you were my baby. I don't think many people really understood that. About three weeks after you left for the Bridge, Daddy and I went out to eat. I saw a girl holding a new-born baby. I could see the love in her eyes for that little soul she was holding. I knew exactly what she felt. I started to cry so hard, Spunk.

I had never missed you so much as at that moment. All my feelings for you just came rushing back. You were my baby in every sense of the word. I was your mother. I still am your mother and will always be your mother.

I will be with you again, Spunk. I want you to be happy while you wait for me, okay? The next time we see each other is the next time we'll never have to say good-bye. I love you so much, Spunk. Be a good boy, okay? Keep helping Mommy and Daddy. We need your soul to watch over us and keep us strong. Give Great Grandma a big kiss for me. Now go and play. Mommy will be okay. I promise.

I love you more than life itself,
Mommy

Robin Pasquazzi
Owner, Petline Casket Company
Greenville, Rhode Island

Some of my best leading men have been dogs and horses.

—Elizabeth Taylor

— Photo by Frank Spear

SUNSHINE BOY

POMERANIAN
8-YEAR-OLD MALE
UNKNOWN - APRIL 29, 1999

Dear Precious Sunny,

My little ray of sunshine. You came to me so sick and mistreated, even the vet was not sure you would ever have a coat of fur again from the terrible case of mange you suffered with. But you did manage to get a beautiful full red coat and were truly a beautiful boy. Always happy and playing and such a brave little four-and-a-half pound bundle. You were full of life and so happy, and you had your little yipping bark that told me you wanted to go out or wanted dinner.

When your Daddy died in February of this year you never left Mommy's side. You were my comfort and my joy. Sleeping on my legs every night and staying under my chair all during the day. Not wanting me out of your sight ever.

Then the most terrible thing happened and the stereo speaker tumbled off the bookcase and I turned to see you on the floor bleeding and convulsing from being hit by it. I was frantic and tried to do all I could, but my sweet little boy, you were gone in just minutes.

I love you so much, and I miss you so much. My ray of sunshine was gone and now I have to try and say good-bye to you. This is the hardest thing I have had to do since your human daddy died. I only hope he found you and you are now comforting him for me until we can all be together again someday. You can sleep in Daddy's legs now and give your love to him from me.

I love you, Sunny Boy, and I miss you so much. Please stay with Daddy and wait for me. I will be with you again. I only hope you didn't feel fear in those last moments of your life, because you were such a brave little baby.

Love always,
Mommy and the rest of the furkids, who miss you too.

Sandra Wentzel
Wimauma, Florida

TERI ANN

LABRADOR MIX
16-YEAR-OLD FEMALE
JANUARY 1, 1983 - MAY 15, 1999

Well, I guess this is it. I know that you have given me the best sixteen years. You have always been by my side no matter what is going on in life. For this I am truly blessed. I always wondered if I would ever be able to say good-bye to you, my little girl...but I guess I can't. So I decided to write you.

I wanted you to understand that this decision was made out of total love for you...not from a selfish side of me. If that was the truth, you would still feel pain. I know now that you don't, and that you will be in good hands with Popadopulus. I know that his hands are reaching out to take you home with him. Do me one thing...lick him for me.

You may be out of my sight and out of my ability to touch you...but you will never be out of my heart. I will always feel you and I know that with the special bond we have, you will always be by my side.

I have learned a lot from you. I learned to become an achiever, not a quitter. I know that when the ache in my heart goes away I will have learned from you once more. You have always given to me without any expectations, your loyalty. And I know that was because you loved me. I want you to know that I love you too. You have had such an impact on so many people. I hope that someday I will have made an impact on someone, too.

You have been much more than a dog to me. You are my little girl. I will take you wherever I go, and when I pass from this earth I will have our remains put together. I know that you must go now from me, but I will find you again one day. Know that I love you so very much!

May God give you...
for every storm, a rainbow,
for every tear, a smile,
for every care, a promise,
and a blessing in each trial.
For every problem life sends,
a faithful friend to share,
for every sigh, a sweet song,
and an answer for each prayer.

—an Irish blessing

REST IN PEACE!!
X O X O X O X O X O

Tracy Ann Boyle
Registered Nurse
Lackawanna, New York

TEXAS LAD
"CHOACH"

COLLIE/ROUGH
14-YEAR-OLD MALE
FEBRUARY 14, 1985 - MAY 22, 1999

Choach,

This is for you, my gallant Collie. Always by my side, ready to protect me, love me, guide me through whatever challenge came our way.

Fourteen years is a long time my friend, and every one has been good for us. Texas Lad they called you, and it sounded good to some, but you and I know you liked Choach much better.

I know that you hung on all week just so I could get used to the idea of you being gone, and for that I thank you. I know you were tired and out of fight. Things happen so fast, and I think you were just giving me a little time to adjust. As always, thinking of me, and not your own pain.

I'll not cry anymore my friend, for you must be in a better place and Casey, your mate, has been waiting for you there.

Myself, I have faith that I will run with you both one day.

I love you dearly, my friend, and thank you for the years you gave me. Those I will never forget.

Love you, my pup.

Patricia J. Mann
Pre-Press Technician
Kirby, Texas

Everything that lives, lives not alone nor for itself.

—William Blake

WATSON

AIREDALE/LABRADOR MIX
12-YEAR-OLD MALE
DECEMBER 1988 - MARCH 26, 2000

To Our Beloved Watson,

You have been such a huge part of our lives for eleven years, and we miss you SO much. We trust you are out of pain and at peace now in the place that God has especially for animals.

We love you more than we can say, and it has broken our hearts to see you take ill so quickly and look at us so trustingly when the going got tough for you and we had to make the hardest decision of all — to put you to sleep once your illness was diagnosed as terminal. We had hoped that you might recover, but this did not happen and you were relying on us.

It was very tough watching you in your last minutes, but we're glad we could hold you and talk to you as you lapsed into unconsciousness and then breathed your last. We did this because we loved you so — which seems so strange, when we are called upon to save lives upon this earth.

Thank you for the huge amount of joy and laughter you brought to us all. Thank you for your unconditional love and huge welcomes whenever we came home — we miss that all so much now. There is a big gap which you had filled, and you will long be remembered, dear beloved Watson — the dog who talked. Gone from the home, but not from our hearts.

Hugs and pats from your everloving
Margot, Ray, Mia and Ross

Margot Howard
School Secretary
Pakuranga, Auckland, New Zealand

YOGI BEAR

LHASA APSO
13-YEAR-OLD MALE
AUGUST 25, 1985 - SEPTEMBER 22, 1998

Dear Yogi Bear,

It seems impossible that you have been gone for so long. Sometimes it seems like yesterday that we lost you.

Congestive heart disease is such a terrible thing. Your lungs kept filling with fluid, and you struggled so much for breath. But I still didn't have the courage to end your suffering. I didn't think I would ever be able to make that decision, and that is why I held you every night and asked God to take you, and I told you it was okay to go to Heaven. But the day you couldn't walk, I couldn't stand to see you suffer anymore. The look in your eyes told me what I had to do.

I try not to think about those last few moments that nearly tore my heart out. We did what we thought was best for you, little angel. As Mike and I held you one last time, I kept thinking this couldn't really be happening, but I knew it was something that had to be done for you because nobody in the whole world loves you as much as I do, Yogi. As you quietly took your last breath, the struggle ended and you were at peace. I knew you had gone on to a better place.

I still cry a lot, but I really am doing better each and every day. I cannot allow myself to dwell on your death, and I am trying really hard to celebrate your life. You surely did love life!!! How many times did I catch you running with the end of the toilet paper. The more I yelled, the funnier you thought it was!

Your buddy, Boo Boo, has had a rough time without you, but he seems to be doing better these days. He missed you so much and was so afraid to be left alone. I guess he thought we may never come home, and he would lose us just like he lost you, his very best friend.

We named the puppy Yogi's Shadow. Looking at him is like seeing a miniature of you, Yogi! I truly believe you sent him to all of us to help ease the pain. You must be whispering in his ear and helping him along, because he does so many things you used to do! Shadow has helped us remember your life as you grew up with us.

Wait for me, my little angel. One day we will be together again. Until that time, take a deep breath and run like the wind, Yogi Bear!!! I have prayed that God will give you a kiss for me.

I love you,
Terri

Terri Szczecina
Homemaker
Century, Florida

YOGIE BIERRA

HUSKY/SHEPHERD/LABRADOR MIX
14-YEAR-OLD MALE
MARCH 1984 - MARCH 25, 1998

My Precious Puppy,

This is so hard. It breaks my heart and burns my soul. I've put it off as long as I could. But I can't stand to see you suffer. The medicine isn't working any longer. And this is the only other way I can help you.

I love you. I love you more than you will ever know. You are such a special boy. The first dog that was truly mine. What a cute puppy you were! How could anyone not love you? We had many good years together. You gave me such joy. I never get tired of seeing your puppy face. I never realized you were getting old. I refused to see your body aging, growing frail and weak.

I can't imagine my life without you. I know a part of me will die with you. I will love you forever. Soon you will be leaving me. Going on to another life. I cannot come. You must go by yourself. Don't be afraid when you wake up and I am not there. It will be okay. Buffy Lee will be there for you. You will be pain free. You'll be free—young and strong again. You'll run and play. There will be lots of animals for you to play with.

Please don't forget me. Remember I won't be far away. You and Buffer can come back home—if you want to. There will be many times I will call for you. Please come to me.

Close your eyes ... Go to sleep my baby ... Go to sleep....

Sandy

Sandy Wantuch
Dental Assistant
South Bend, Indiana

—I wrote this letter to Yogie and attached it to his pillow that went with him to the vet's and was cremated with him ... Sandy

I think that dogs are the most amazing creatures;
they give unconditional love.
For me they are the role model for being alive.

— Gilda Radner

Other Friends

We are part of the earth and it is part of us.
The perfumed flowers are our sisters;
the deer, the horse, the great eagle,
these are our brothers.
All things are connected like the blood
which unites one's family.

—Chief Seattle

CASPER

AFRICAN GRAY PARROT
18-YEAR-OLD FEMALE
1981 - JULY 17, 1999

My Dearest Casper,

I will miss you until we meet again! Your voice was mine, and I don't know what to do without you!

Fly to the Bridge! I love you!!!

Nancy Miramontes
Tattoo-A-Pet Agent
Woodland Hills, California

*Without birds, where would we have learned
that there can be song in the heart?*

—Hal Borland

— Photo by Frank Spear

CHICKEN BAXTER

HATCH/KELSO GAME HEN
FEMALE
UNKNOWN - NOVEMBER 26, 1998

Hi Sweetie:

I wanted to write to you to tell you that I miss you and that I'm so sad and sorry that you died. I know that you realized how much I loved you, but you were just too terrified to ever let a person touch you again after all the abuse you had been through at the hands of people. I'm so sorry that I didn't realize how sick you were and what was wrong with you. I thought you were egg bound and, because you never came down from your roost in the oleanders, I couldn't see how swollen your throat was. I wish so much that you had come down before the day you died. I could have saved you and you could have still been living here in my yard. I could still be able to call for you and say, "Hi good girl, want some corn?" and you could come running or flying over to me and eat your food. I miss you so much, honey. You were my precious little Chicken girl. You were such a good girl; so sweet and pretty and so very intelligent and responsive.

How I wish I could have made your life wonderful to make up for all the abuse you took at the hands of the people who didn't love you. I used to hear your distress crying in your cage, and I would pray for you that you would be all right. I didn't even know what you looked like then because I couldn't see through the bushes. When you found your way into my yard after they had abandoned you, I saw what a beautiful chicken you were. Your pretty little tiny head was so dainty with its tiny little comb on top. All the multicolors of brown and beige on your feathers made you look like you were composed of brown lace. Your beautiful black and brown long tail feathers were so pretty too. You were such a beautiful and wonderful girl, and I loved you so very much.

All I wanted to do was to give you a happy life full of freedom and free from all stress and abuse. I tried to find information about you at the feed stores but the books were mostly about raising chickens for food. They didn't discuss the problems a free roaming chicken could encounter. Any advice I was able to get was strictly second hand as you could not tolerate letting me get close enough to touch you. I respected that. I knew all you had been through. I knew you could never forget no matter how kind I was to you. You had been through too much.

You were such a good mommy to your eggs that you laid. If I would have just known that you had laid a nest of eggs back in the bushes, you still might be alive today. The man on the internet helped me to learn that was what was going on when you weren't coming out to eat. And then the little kitten got lost in the bushes and was crying. When we found her, we found you on your nest so far back in the oleanders we never would have found you if the little kitten hadn't gotten stuck back there. You were almost starved to death from being so devoted to never leave your nest with its little dried-out, infertile eggs. You were such a wonderful mommy to those eggs, honey.

We were so grateful the little kitten showed us the way to your hidden nest so we could save your life. We took your eggs away so you could be free to leave your nest and resume eating, but the man didn't tell me that I should make sure you didn't eat a lot of food during the early time when you came back out. You were so starving and thin. I fed you as much as you could hold. You were so happy to be eating again. I never knew that feeding you like that was going to cause your death.

I enjoyed feeding you so much, my precious girl, because you loved to eat and it made me so happy to see you really excited about your food and getting to eat. It distressed me when you stopped coming down from your roosting area. I was worried that you were afraid of a cat that had chased you. I missed seeing you pecking around in the yard. I began feeding the cat so he would leave you alone and I tried to find a way to get food up to you until you weren't afraid to come down anymore. Then the man at the feed store said you might be egg bound. So I made a nest box and hung it up in the bushes as best I could, by your roosting area, hoping you would use it, but you didn't. You just stayed up in the bushes, and it was hard to even see you because you were up so high and in so deep. I finally found a way to get food and water balanced way up there, and you would eat and drink, but only a tiny bit each day. I didn't know that you had food stuck in your throat and that you could barely swallow! I even made special foods for you to try to tempt you to eat. It horrifies me now to know that you were starving to death with me putting food in front of you constantly! I'm so sorry, my precious girl.

Finally, the day you died, you came down from your roost. I was able to see how thin you had become. I also saw how swollen your neck was, and I e-mailed to my chicken expert immediately. I stayed with you outside the entire day. I kept shading you from the sun, and I kept the kitten from bothering or trying to play with you. How I wish my advisor would have gotten back to me earlier. By the time I found out what was wrong with you, you were already down on the ground in a coma and all the vets were closed.

My precious girl, please forgive me for allowing you to die like that. You deserved so much better. You deserved to live like a queen after all you had been through. But you didn't get to have that. I'm so very sorry.

How I have missed you over the months since you died, my sweet little girl. I cried so many tears, and being out in the yard has never been the same. Sometimes I think I can still see your little eyes peeking out at me from the bushes.

I found the neck feather. I found it three weeks after you died. I was in my bedroom doing my stretching after my exercises, and I found it on the floor. How beautiful and tiny and perfect it was. I know it couldn't have come in on the bottom of a shoe. It was too perfect and unruffled. There was no way it could have come into my house so long after you were gone. I took it as a message from you or God that you had forgiven me and that you were finally OK and happy. They say a feather is a letter from a bird. Thank you for your letter, Chicken. It helped me so very much.

After you died I found out that you loved me as if I was one of your own little baby chicks that you never got to have. You always made a soft purring sound when I would talk to you. You never clucked around me. How I wish I would have learned while you were still alive that this sound is what chickens make to their baby chicks! You were my baby chick, too.

I look forward to seeing you again someday. I believe you are in heaven waiting for me. Chicken, I love you so very much. Thank you for coming into my life. Be a good girl, and I know that you will until we are together once again.

Love,
Mommy

Chris Baxter
Homemaker
Phoenix, Arizona

To everything there is a season,
and a time to every purpose under heaven:
a time to be born and a time to die.

—Ecclesiasticus 3:1

CLINT

ZEBRA FINCH
13-YEAR-OLD MALE
1985 - APRIL 29, 1998

Clint,

Today, a year ago, was your last day on Earth with me. I knew you were dying when you flew back to the nest, looked at your two-week-old babies and told them good-bye. Somehow I like to think that you also told them you were giving their care over to their mom, Sheri, and to their Grammy.

As I picked you up, your little heart was pounding, and you were breathing so heavily. I knew the end was near for you. I held you in my hand, saw you so valiantly trying to stay with me, but as your body shook, your soul left for that beautiful place of peace.

As you died, I made a promise: "Clint, I promise you I will take care of your babies."

My son, I have kept that promise every day since then. It will always be kept as my last gift of love to you.

Gail McMahon
Editorial Assistant
Birmingham, Alabama

Our task must be to free ourselves
by widening our circle of compassion
to embrace all living creatures.

—Albert Einstein

MISTY

DWARF RABBIT
2-YEAR-OLD FEMALE
JUNE 1997 - MAY 10, 1999

Dear Misty,

I know I was never as good of an owner as I could have been or should have been. I am going to miss the way you would always stand on your hind legs in your cage to beg for treats. You were the greatest bunny ever, and I will never forget you.

You were so young to go. I wish there was something I could have done. Yesterday I was planning on making you some new toys...but today you're gone. I was going to build you a beautiful hutch...but now you're gone.

I know you're happy where you are now. Rainbow Bridge must be beautiful, and I hope that when the time comes to meet again, you will be waiting for me at that beautiful bridge so we can run along the meadows together. I just wish there was something I could have done ... Misty, my baby. I will love you forever and I will never forget you.

> Love forever,
> Jenna
> and the animals ...
> Abaris the horse
> Zantac the cat
> Pamelor the cat
> Ceclor the cat
> Cassie the dog
> Mandy the dog
> Twix the rat

Jenna Stern
Student, age 14
Chapel Hill, North Carolina

We are united to all life.
From this knowledge comes our
spiritual relationship with the universe...
Until he extends the circle of his compassion
to all living things, man himself will not find peace.

—Albert Schweitzer

MOUSE

STANDARD DONKEY
30+-YEAR-OLD FEMALE
UNKNOWN - DECEMBER 24, 1994

Dear Mouse,

You came to us so unexpectedly. And you left too soon.

You needed a new home because your friend was unable to care for you after her surgery, so you came to live with us. You were our first donkey, but not to be our last. We loved to watch you trot through the tall pasture grass, take big juicy bites from apples and listen to you bray. You woke us every morning (and probably the neighbors as well).

You loved your dog-friend, Chance, and he loved you. As your hearing failed and your eyesight gave way to cataracts, remember how Chance would run out into the pasture and circle you, barking, to let you know it was time to eat? You'd rest your chin on his tail and follow him in a slow and patient procession back to your stall. It was a daily ritual and a heartwarming one. You were special to all of us...

...Even when you ignored the vegetable garden for the entire summer, and then finally went through the fence one evening and ate every ear of corn. How you knew that we'd planned to harvest it the very next day is beyond me. We didn't mind, though, because we knew you enjoyed every kernel.

Then came the midnight vet visits in the pasture by flashlight, the blood tests and the medicines. We tried our best to keep you with us longer, but you were shutting down, preparing to leave. The vet estimated your age at thirty-plus years. We'd had you just a little longer than two years. Such a short time to know you, but plenty long enough to love you.

The produce boys at the grocery store always saved boxes of apples for you. How you loved those daily treats! Your last gifts to them, about one week before Christmas, were stockings with candy, gift certificates and your photograph. They liked that.

One week later, you were gone. They asked about you. We told them that we'd found your body early Christmas morning. We had brought you your breakfast of warm homemade bran mash with applesauce and vitamins, which we'd hand-fed you toward the end.

You were a special girl, Mouse. The only way I was able to accept your death was when Mark pointed out to me that Christmas was a fitting time for you to leave because for many years before you came to us, you carried Mary in the church's annual Christmas pageant. You were The Christmas Donkey for many people. And now you are our Christmas Star.

Just days before you left us, I happened to discover a donkey rescue group. We became members and now support the rescue of abused and neglected donkeys. We do this with you in our hearts and minds, Mouse. Thank you for letting us know and love you. And thank you for leading us to help other donkeys.

Always,
Laura

In spite of all the barriers and divisions
that prejudice and superstition
have heaped up between the human and the nonhuman,
we may take it as certain that, in the long run,
as we treat our fellow beings, "the animals,"
so shall we treat our fellow men.

—Henry S. Salt

PRANCER

QUARTER HORSE/ARABIAN
12-YEAR-OLD GELDING
1987 - MAY 28, 1999

Prancer,

I love you. We will miss you, but you are in a better place with no pain. I will see you again, and we will dance and prance in the clouds. 'Til then baby, all my love...

Beth Wallace
Landscaper
Clarksville, Tennessee

Perhaps they are not the stars, but rather openings
in Heaven where the love of our lost ones pours through
and shines down upon us to let us know that they are happy.

—Eskimo legend

RUDY

SUN CONURE PARROT
UNKNOWN - JUNE 5, 1999

Dear Rudy,

I can't believe you are gone. Wherever you are — I love you still and miss you so much I can hardly breathe. My shoulder where you sat feels bare. I need to feel you snuggle up to me. I miss your laugh and squawk. I thought we would be together for many more years. When you flew away to Heaven you took part of me with you ...

Without you, there'll be no Sun in my life. My heart flies with you ... wherever you are.

Love,
Mommy

Cathy Jackson
Wantage, New Jersey

May the footprints we leave behind
show that we've walked in kindness
toward the earth
and every living thing.

—Inspired by American Indian Philosophy

SEI ABU SEYN

ARABIAN HORSE
28-YEAR-OLD STALLION
JUNE 26, 1968 - DECEMBER 13, 1996

I have so many memories.

It took me ten years to get you, my dream horse. I could still kill the people who abused you so long ago. But, as I never forgot you, you never forgot me. We were given eighteen wonderful years together.

Your love and trust got me through the most difficult part of my life. You taught me that I could love and trust again. If you could, so could I. You were so gallant and gentle, but always proud. You were my heart and soul, every little girl's dream come true. Oh, my proud horse...I wish I could have given you the babies and the heritage you deserved to leave behind. One day we will play in the lovely golden light again. Until then, may God hold you in the hollow of His hand. I will love you until forever.

Claire

Claire Newbre
Horse and Dog Breeder
Lindsay, California

Until one has loved an animal,
a part of one's soul remains unawakened.

—Anatole France

YOSHI

HAMSTER
2½-YEAR-OLD MALE
JANUARY 1997 - JULY 7, 1999

I couldn't have asked for a sweeter, friendlier little guy to come into my life than you. I'll never forget the clever little things you did... escaping off my bed by sliding down the sheets, begging for lettuce, stuffing your cheek pouches with food and munching as you slept in your nest. I'll be keeping your exercise wheel to remember you by (as though I could forget you).

Putting you to sleep was one of the hardest things I've ever done. I was terrified that it was the wrong decision, but when the vet told me you were dying of cancer, I realized that it was the right choice. I couldn't let you suffer, not after the long and happy life you'd led. My other friends will help to fill the emptiness inside, but they'll never be able to replace you. Everyone in the family will miss you...even the ones who thought you were "just a rodent." They loved you too, but not as much as I do.

You are in my heart.

Kerry Gallo
Student, age 17
Cumming, Georgia

The greatness of a nation and its moral progress
can be judged by the way its animals are treated.

—Mohandas Gandhi

— Photo by Robi Walch

"Love the animals: God has given them the rudiments of
thought and joy untroubled. Do not trouble their joy,
don't harass them, don't deprive them of their happiness,
don't work against God's intent."

—Dostoevsky

I like pigs.
Dogs look up to us.
Cats look down on us.
Pigs treat us as equals.

—Winston Churchill

— Photo by Frank Spear

*I have perceived that to be
with those I like is enough.*

—Walt Whitman

Mercy to all animals means mercy to mankind.

—Henry Bergh

My Forever Friend

I know it must be different now that I am no longer here.
I can see how much I was loved and how all of you did care.
It will be hard at first when you look around for me,
hoping to find me lying on the bed
or outside beside my favorite tree.
But someday what you will begin to see,
although it'll take some time,
is that you brought happiness to me,
and forever it will be mine.
Remember it's the family I had
that meant the most to me,
so please don't be sad,
it was just my time to leave.

—author unknown

The author with Baci

Proceeds from the sale of this book will be donated to Animal Welfare.